THE
LITURGICAL
MINISTRY
SERIES®

D1495572

GUIDE FOR EXTRAORDINARY MINISTERS OF HOLY COMMUNION

SECOND EDITION

Corinna Laughlin
Kenneth A. Riley
Paul Turner

LTP
LITURGY
TRAINING
PUBLICATIONS

Nihil Obstat
Very Reverend Daniel A. Smilanic, JCD
Vicar for Canonical Services
Archdiocese of Chicago
May 1, 2013

Imprimatur
Reverend Monsignor John F. Canary, STL, DMIN
Vicar General
Archdiocese of Chicago
May 1, 2013

THE LITURGICAL MINISTRY SERIES®: GUIDE FOR EXTRAORDINARY MINISTERS
OF HOLY COMMUNION, SECOND EDITION © 2013 Archdiocese of Chicago:
Liturgy Training Publications, 3949 South Racine Avenue, Chicago IL 60609;
1-800-933-1800, fax 1-800-933-7094, e-mail orders@ltp.org. All rights reserved.
See our website at www.LTP.org.

Cover and interior photos © John Zich.

Printed in the United States of America.

19 18 17 16 15   2 3 4 5 6

Library of Congress Control Number: 2013933434

ISBN 978-1-61671-128-3

ELEMC2

Anima Christi
Prayer to the Most Holy Redeemer

Soul of Christ, sanctify me.
Body of Christ, save me.
Blood of Christ, embolden me.
Water from the side of Christ, wash me.
Passion of Christ, strengthen me.
O good Jesus, hear me.
Within your wounds hide me.
Never permit me to be parted from you.
From the evil Enemy defend me.
At the hour of my death call me
and bid me come to you,
that with your Saints I may praise you
for age upon age.
Amen.

Table of Contents

Preface

Give them some food yourselves.

—Mark 6:37a

"Give them some food yourselves,"[1] Jesus said. It was an extraordinary command, an impossible command. His disciples had followed him to a deserted place, but a vast crowd still managed to find them. The crowd was hungry for God. The heart of Jesus was moved with pity. But his disciples were moved with despair.

It was getting late. The disciples were probably getting hungry. They only had a snack — five loaves and two fish, not nearly enough to share with a throng. They probably didn't have enough energy either. So they came up with a practical suggestion and presented it to Jesus. "Dismiss them," they said, "so that they can go to the surrounding farms and villages and buy themselves something to eat."[2]

It wasn't a bad proposal. It expressed their care and concern. It made sense to the disciples under the circumstances. But Jesus — not always known for practicality — had another idea.

"Give them some food yourselves."[3]

The disciples were not just short on food. They were short on cash. "Are we to buy two hundred days' wages worth of food and give it to them to eat?"[4] they asked. They weren't envisioning a gourmet picnic in the desert. The size of the crowd was just enormous.

Jesus stuck with his plan. He took what little food they had, blessed it, broke it, and gave it to the *disciples* — not to the people. The disciples had to give them the food themselves.

And, miraculously, there was enough.[5]

This story foreshadows another miracle, the gift of the Eucharist. Just as Jesus took, blessed, broke, and gave bread in a "deserted place,"[6] so he took, blessed, broke, and gave bread at the Last Supper. Just as he fed those who hungered, so he feeds us with his Body and Blood. Just as he gave the bread and fish to the disciples, who then gave them to the people, so the Church entrusts the Body and Blood of Christ to ministers, who then give them to the faithful.

NOTES

1. Mark 6:37a.

2. Ibid., 6:36.

3. Ibid., 6:37a.

4. Ibid., 6:37b.

5. See Ibid., 6:34–44.

6. Ibid., 6:31.

Welcome

You have agreed to serve the Church as an extraordinary minister of Holy Communion during Mass and with those who are sick and home-bound. In doing so, you take your place in a long line of disciples who enjoyed the company of Jesus, listened to his word, wondered about his commands, cared for his people, and did what he asked.

This ministry puts you at the center of the Church's life. The celebration of the Eucharist on the Lord's Day is our most important activity. We gather on the day of the Resurrection to express our belief in eternal life. We listen to the Word of God. We give thanks for life and salvation.

At Mass some people will bring the bread and wine to the sanctuary so that the priest may *take* it. All of us pray silently with him while he *blesses* it. We reflect on the community we share and the sacrifice we make as he *breaks* it and pours it. And you will help him as he *gives* it to the people.

When faithful believers participate at Mass, they look forward to receiving Holy Communion. You will be there. You will be a servant of Christ fulfilling his will to feed the hungry, by giving them something to eat and drink.

You already know the importance of Mass and Holy Communion. The Eucharist sums up our beliefs: that there is a God, that God's Word took flesh in Jesus, that the Holy Spirit continues to guide the Church, that God speaks to us through the Scriptures, that Jesus worked miracles, that he gave us his Body and Blood on the night before he died, and that he rose from the dead on the third day. When we gather for the Eucharist as the Body of Christ, we place our lives in God's hands. We respond in faith to the revelation we have received.

> ✛ The celebration of Mass . . . is the center of the whole of Christian life for the Church both universal and local, as well as for each of the faithful individually.
> — *General Instruction of the Roman Missal, 16*

In the Mass, God sanctifies the world in Christ, and humanity worships the Father through the Son in the Holy Spirit.

The diversity of ministers is essential to the fruitful celebration of the Mass. All of the faithful are summoned to a "full, conscious, and active participation"[1] that burns with faith, hope, and charity, by reason of their Baptism.[2]

The Church depends on extraordinary ministers of Holy Communion (hereafter, often shortened to extraordinary minister[s]) for this purpose. They fulfill one of the ministries that helps the proper arrangement of the Mass. When all the ministers fulfill their functions with individual integrity in service to the whole, the mystery of the Eucharist is revealed more clearly.

Your love for Christ draws you to the Eucharist. Your love for the Church draws you to liturgical service. As an extraordinary minister, you are integral to the sacramental sharing that is the highlight of the Mass.

At the miracle of the loaves and fishes, Jesus wanted to feed the multitude, and he commanded his disciples to give them something to eat. At the Last Supper he commanded those same disciples to eat and drink his body and blood. The extraordinary minister serves at the will of Christ and the Church to serve the Communion that sanctifies the people of God.

About This Book

This book will help you in several ways. It aims to inform, advise, and inspire you in this service. You will learn more about this ministry — what the Church asks of you and why it is important. You will receive some counsel on doing it well — how to perform this ministry during the Communion Rite of the Mass and how to give Holy Communion to those who are sick or homebound. You will also find avenues for spiritual enrichment — how to pray to God and serve the community throughout the week in ways that deepen your ministry at Sunday Mass.

About the Authors

This book was written by three authors. Paul Turner wrote the first sections of the book: the "Preface," "Theology and History of the Extraordinary Minister of Holy Communion," and "Spirituality and Formation of the Extraordinary Minister of Holy Communion." He is the pastor of St. Anthony Parish in Kansas City, Missouri. A priest of the Diocese of Kansas City–St. Joseph, he holds a doctorate in sacred theology from Sant' Anselmo in Rome. He is the author of many pastoral resources about sacraments and the liturgy.

Corinna Laughlin and Kenneth A. Riley wrote the practical explanation of the extraordinary minister's duties in "Serving as an Extraordinary Minister of Holy Communion" and "Frequently Asked Questions" and have provided the book's resource section and glossary.

Corinna Laughlin is the director of liturgy for St. James Cathedral in Seattle. She also serves on the Liturgical Commission for the Archdiocese of Seattle. She co-authored *The Liturgical Ministry Series: Guide for Sacristans* and *The Liturgical Ministry Series: Guide for Servers* (both LTP), and is a frequent contributor to *Sourcebook for Sundays, Seasons, and Weekdays: The Almanac for Parish Liturgy*. Corinna has also written articles for *Pastoral Liturgy, Today's Liturgy, Ministry & Liturgy,* and AIM. She holds a doctorate in English from the University of Washington and a bachelor's degree in English from Mount Holyoke College.

Fr. Riley is Judicial Vicar, Moderator of the Curia, and Vice Chancellor for Canonical Affairs in Kansas City, Missouri, and serves as a member of the Canon Law Society of America's clergy committee. Also a priest of the Diocese of Kansas City–St. Joseph, he holds a master of arts in theology and a licentiate in canon law from The Catholic University of America in Washington, D.C.

Questions for Discussion and Reflection

1. Why have you agreed to serve as an extraordinary minister of Holy Communion?

_____

_____

_____

_____

_____

2. What do you hope to gain in your understanding of the theology and function of the ministry through this book?

_____

_____

_____

_____

_____

NOTES

1. *Constitution on the Sacred Liturgy* (CSL), 14.

2. See *General Instruction of the Roman Missal* (GIRM), 17–18.

Theology and History of the Extraordinary Minister of Holy Communion

The God of power and Father of our Lord Jesus Christ / has freed you from sin / and brought you to new life / through water and the Holy Spirit. / He now anoints you with the chrism of salvation, / so that, united with his people, / you may remain for ever a member of Christ / who is Priest, Prophet, and King.

— Rite of Baptism for Children, 62

Baptism: The Foundation of Ministry

Baptism is the foundation of all ministry in the Church. Before you are an extraordinary minister, you are a baptized member of the Body of Christ, with all the attendant blessings and duties.

Baptism helps you personally: it cleanses you from sin and incorporates you into the Body of Christ. Baptism also gives you responsibilities toward others: it assigns you a place among the faithful who worship at the Eucharist and who serve their neighbor in the name of Christ. Baptism summons you to worship and service.

Who You Are

As a believer, your role at Mass is so important that, together with others at church, you are called a priestly people. All the faithful join with the celebrant to give thanks to God and offer the sacrifice. In doing this, they also learn to offer themselves completely to God.[1] The law about going to Mass on Sunday is not to "attend" Mass, but to "participate" at Mass.[2] All the baptized have something to do there. It is not just the priest who offers — all the priestly people offer themselves, offer the sacrifice, and share the communion.

We become a priestly people at Baptism. During the ceremony, a child is anointed on the crown of the head with chrism, while the deacon or priest says, "The God of power and Father of our Lord Jesus Christ / has freed you from sin / and brought you to new life / through water and the Holy Spirit. / He now anoints you with the chrism of salvation, / so that, united with his people, / you may remain for ever a member of Christ / who is Priest, Prophet, and King."[3]

We become a priestly people at Baptism.

Christians are anointed into the ministry of Christ as leaders. Our participation at Mass is priestly. "The faithful indeed, by virtue of their royal priesthood, share in the offering of the Eucharist."[4] They do so in other ways as well: "They exercise that priesthood, too, by the reception of the sacraments, by prayer and thanksgiving, by the witness of a holy life, self-denial and active charity."[5]

Baptism seals us for worship and marks us as children of God. Because it is received only once, Baptism imparts a special character for this purpose. "Incorporated into the Church by Baptism, the faithful are appointed by their baptismal character to christian religious worship."[6]

> ✠ The faithful indeed, by virtue of their royal priest-hood, share in the offering of the Eucharist.
>
> — *Lumen gentium*, 10

The *Catechism of the Catholic Church* has these passages in mind when it says, "Incorporated into the Church by Baptism, the faithful have received the sacramental character that consecrates them for Christian religious worship (cf. LG, 11). The baptismal seal enables and commits Christians to serve God by a vital participation in the holy liturgy of the Church and to exercise their baptismal priesthood by the witness of holy lives and practical charity (cf. LG, 10)."[7]

Marked for worship, the faithful are also set apart for service. At Confirmation, the baptized receive the fullness of the Holy Spirit. The Spirit comes with spiritual gifts, intending us to use them.

> "Christ gives varied gifts to his Church, and the Spirit distributes them among the members of Christ's Body to build up the holy people of God in unity and love. Be active

members of the Church, alive in Jesus Christ. Under the guidance of the Holy Spirit give your lives completely in the service of all, as did Christ, who came not to be served but to serve."[8]

This service takes many forms, as the Holy Spirit's gifts do. We care for the sick; we educate the youth; we bring relief to the traumatized; we advocate for life. The service we offer is not a merely humanitarian effort. It serves the mission of the Church. It proclaims the reign of God. The command of Jesus to love our neighbor motivates us to service. When we act on what we believe with the intention to do God's will, our deeds proclaim to others the Good News of salvation.

> ✠ Under the guidance of the Holy Spirit give your lives completely in the service of all, as did Christ, who came not to be served but to serve.
>
> — *Rite of Confirmation, 22*

The baptized proclaim the Gospel in all circumstances: "Reborn as sons and daughters of God, they must profess publicly the faith they have received from God through the church."[9] But they do this in a special way at the Mass. "Both in the offering [sacrifice] and in holy Communion, in their separate ways, though not indiscriminately, all have their own part to play in the liturgical action."[10]

Besides participating at Mass the faithful have other responsibilities as well. They should develop a religious sense, an inner piety. They should show charity toward the brothers and sisters with whom they share the Eucharist.[11] In short, they show on the outside the faith they hold on the inside.

Believers also show that faith when they perform some specific responsibility at the liturgy. "The faithful, moreover, should not refuse to serve the People of God in gladness whenever they are asked to perform some particular service or function in the celebration."[12]

Everyone participates at Mass on some level. All sing the songs, make the responses, proclaim the Creed, and observe moments of silence. But your task as an extraordinary minister at Mass is one example of service to the people of God in the celebration of the Mass.

During the Liturgy of the Eucharist, extraordinary ministers assist the smooth execution of the distribution of Holy Communion. They do this only in the last part of the service, but they participate throughout as a member of the priestly people.

Extraordinary ministers also bring the sacrament to those who are sick and homebound. In this way those who are unable to participate in Sunday Mass with the entire assembly can still share in the communion of sacrament and friendship.

Ideally, the extraordinary minister attends Mass first and then brings Holy Communion immediately from the bread and wine consecrated at that Mass to the sick. This makes the connection between Mass and Holy Communion more deliberate. Those who are unable physically to attend are drawn into the mystery of Sunday's gathering by their sharing in the very Holy Communion offered to the faithful at Mass.

In this case, the extraordinary minister is not helping with the smooth distribution of Holy Communion but is more personally the one who connects the sick person to Sunday worship. The minister leads a short prayer service in which the Scriptures of Sunday may be proclaimed. The Lord's Prayer is recited, and the minister offers Holy Communion to the sick. Usually the minister brings Holy Communion under the form of consecrated bread, but if the sick person has trouble chewing, Holy Communion may be administered under the form of consecrated wine.

If the sick person is dying, Holy Communion may be administered under a special form called *Viaticum*, or "food for the journey." Normally administered by a priest, *Viaticum* may be offered to the dying by a lay minister when certain conditions are present.

In these ways can be seen the pastoral care that the Church wishes to extend to the sick and dying. So dearly does the Church desire the communion of the faithful in these circumstances that the sacrament is made more easily available to those in need. The extraordinary minister becomes a vanguard of the Church's mercy.

Extraordinary ministers who visit the same people week after week often develop a special bond with them. They share faith and friendship. Some people who are sick say they don't want to be a bother to anyone, but ministers are usually anxious to make the extra effort, to bring Holy Communion to those who are in need. In their conversation they learn more about the faith they share, the Baptism they have received, their love for the Eucharist, and their willingness to proclaim the gospel of mercy.

Throughout your life God has revealed himself to you in many ways. In faith you have served God in the Church. At Mass you have worshipped as a member of the assembly of the faithful. Now you fulfill part of your baptismal covenant in a specific way, living in faith and serving the Church as an extraordinary minister of Holy Communion.

The History of the Ministry

Extraordinary ministers have been essential to the reverent sharing of Holy Communion, especially when it is distributed under both forms to the faithful. Their ministry was born, though, because of several practical necessities.

Priests and deacons are the ordinary ministers of Holy Communion.

In the early days of the Church, there were fewer restrictions about who distributed Holy Communion. For example, a sick person could have asked a friend to bring the sacrament. One of the early martyrs of the Church, St. Tarcisius, was killed while bringing Holy Communion to the sick as an acolyte. But by the Middle Ages the ministry was restricted to bishops and priests. Deacons were considered the extraordinary ministers of Holy Communion, and on some occasions they administered the Blood of Christ from the chalice. Throughout Christian history, rare circumstances existed when laypeople served as exceptional ministers of Holy Communion, for example in danger of someone's death or in times of persecution. But the practice was largely unknown.

The Second Vatican Council opened up the ministry of distributing Holy Communion. They also changed the use of the word *extraordinary*. Formerly, deacons were extraordinary ministers of Holy Communion. But because deacons are ordained clergy, the Council included them among the *ordinary* ministers of Holy Communion. The Council permitted bishops to appoint laypeople to distribute Communion, and these were now called *extraordinary* ministers. Although many of them are *extraordinary* according to the common definition of someone wonderful and exceptional, the word here means "outside the ordinary," that is, they are not among those in holy orders who, by reason of Ordination, have the responsibility of providing Communion to the faithful.

In 1969, the Vatican announced several reasons for expanding Communion ministry to the laity.

- Outside the Mass, people needed access to Holy Communion when an ordinary minister was not available;

- The usual minister was sometimes impeded by poor health, advanced age, or the demands of the pastoral ministry;

- Sometimes the number of faithful wishing to receive Holy Communion at Mass was so great that the celebration was taking too long.

The reasons all pertained to the great demand for Holy Communion. The shortage of priests was not yet a significant problem. Prior to the twentieth century, very few people received Holy Communion at a typical Sunday Mass. Pope Pius X started promoting regular Holy Communion in 1905, and the practice had caught on. It was this wonderful circumstance that caused the need for extraordinary ministers of Holy Communion: the great desire to receive this sacrament, a desire expressed by more numbers of the faithful than at any other time in history.

Bishops could now appoint ministers to assist with the distribution of Holy Communion from among the laity, provided they were "outstanding in Christian life, in faith, and in morals, and . . . trained to carry out so exalted a function."[13] At first, it was thought that persons of a "mature age" would be ideal, and men more so than women, but these qualifiers were soon lifted.

From the beginning, the vision of this ministry was not limited to distributing Holy Communion during Mass. Laypeople were needed to distribute Holy Communion outside of Mass as well.

When the rites for Anointing the Sick were revised in 1972, they specified that those who were dying could receive Holy Communion from a lay minister.

A more comprehensive instruction on facilitating reception of Holy Communion in certain circumstances appeared in 1973.

> ✠ In case of necessity or with at least the presumed permission of the competent minister, any priest or deacon is to give viaticum, or, if no ordained minister is available any member of the faithful who has been duly appointed.
>
> —*Pastoral Care of the Sick: Rites of Anointing and Viaticum; General Introduction, 29*

"There are several situations in which a shortage of ministers of Holy Communion has been pointed out:

- within Mass because of a great crowd of people or some disability of the celebrant;

- outside Mass when distance makes it difficult to bring Holy Communion, especially as *Viaticum* to the sick in danger of death;

- or when the sheer number of sick people, especially in hospitals or similar institutions, requires several ministers.

"In order, then, that the faithful who are in the state of grace and rightly and devoutly wish to share in the sacred meal may not be deprived of this sacramental aid and solace, Pope Paul VI has decided it opportune to authorize special ministers who will be empowered to give communion to themselves and others of the faithful, under the exact and specified conditions here listed."[14]

"The faithful who are special ministers of communion must be persons whose good qualities of Christian life, faith, and morals recommend them. Let them strive to be worthy of this great office, foster their own devotion to the eucharist, and show an example to the rest of the faithful by their own devotion and reverence toward the most august sacrament of the altar. No one is to be chosen whose appointment the faithful might find disquieting."[15]

A brief rite was then developed to appoint a person to this ministry. The priest or a deacon introduces the candidates to the community. He explains the purpose of their service. Then he asks them these questions:

"Are you resolved to undertake the office of giving the body and blood of the Lord to your brothers and sisters and so serve to build up the Church?"

"Are you resolved to administer the holy eucharist with the utmost care and reverence?"

To each question, the candidates answer, "I am." The celebrant then offers this prayer of blessing:

Merciful Father,
creator and guide of your family,
bless ✚ our brothers and sisters N. and N.

May they faithfully give the bread of life to your people.

Strengthened by this sacrament,
may they come at last to the banquet of heaven.

We ask this through Christ our Lord.
Amen.

Or, he may offer this prayer instead:

Gracious Lord,
you nourish us with the body and blood of your Son,
that we might have eternal life.

Bless ✚ our brothers and sisters who have been chosen
to give the bread of heaven and the cup of salvation
to your faithful people.

May the saving mysteries they distribute
lead them to the joys of eternal life.

We ask this through Christ our Lord.
Amen.[16]

The ceremony concludes with other prayers. If this has taken place at Mass, some of those newly installed may help distribute Holy Communion to the faithful.

At first the change was difficult for many Catholics. For centuries, only a priest would touch the Eucharist with his hands. All communicants received the Body of Christ directly on the tongue. None would even touch the sacred vessels. These practices manifested the deep respect of the faithful for Holy Communion and for the priest. The first extraordinary ministers were men and women of proven character, but also of great courage. Some of them endured the disapproval and anger of their peers. But they forged a ministry that has become broadly welcomed and deemed nearly indispensable in many Catholic parishes around the world.

As the practice developed, the presence of extraordinary ministers expanded one's field of vision at Mass. The Holy Spirit's gifts were becoming more manifest. They appeared in a variety of ministries, and the ministries were working together for the good of the people of God.

Thus, a ministry born of practical necessity was becoming something else — a manifestation of the gifts of the Spirit, an expression of the variety of ministries in the Church, and an opportunity for lay leaders to show the community's respect for the real presence of Christ, as well as its joy in Holy Communion.

The Communion Rite within the Mass

The service of extraordinary ministers fits into the overall structure of the Mass. Within that framework, ministers can find the spiritual heart of their service to the people of God.

We begin Mass with Introductory Rites that offer praise to God and express contrition for our sins. We then hear God's voice in readings from Scripture, and we hear Christ speak to us in his own words in the Gospel. The Homily applies these texts to our lives, and we—the priestly people—offer the Universal Prayer (or Prayer of the Faithful) for the Church and the world.

In the Liturgy of the Eucharist, the gifts of bread and wine are brought to the altar together with our offerings for the Church and the poor. These are symbols of ourselves, signs of our desire to offer our very lives up to God for transformation. During the Eucharistic Prayer, the Holy Spirit transforms the bread and wine into the Body and Blood of Christ, as the Church makes her great act of thanksgiving. Although the priest says most of these words by himself, all the priestly people join with him in silent prayer, making this offering to God.

The Eucharistic Prayer usually follows several steps. It begins with a dialogue between the priest and the people, in which we proclaim our desire to give thanks to God. In the Preface we hear the reasons why we give thanks at this Mass. The Preface may praise God for something relating to the current season (liturgical time) or feast. All sing the "Holy, Holy, Holy" uniting our voices with the choirs of heaven. The priest continues to give reasons for our thanksgiving, and then asks the Holy Spirit to change the bread and wine into the Body and Blood of

Christ. The priest narrates the story of the Last Supper, repeating the words of Jesus, "This is my Body," "This is the chalice of my Blood."[17] All sing an acclamation.

The priest proclaims the Death and Resurrection of Christ, and he offers this sacrifice to God. He prays for the Holy Spirit to come upon the people gathered in faith. He makes petitions for the living and the dead, and he offers a final acclamation of praise, which refers to Jesus Christ: "Through him, and with him, and in him, / O God, almighty Father, / in the unity of the Holy Spirit, / all glory and honor is yours, / for ever and ever." All respond, "Amen." Almost all the Eucharistic Prayers follow this basic structure.

The Communion Rite begins with the Lord's Prayer, a sign of our communion as brothers and sisters under a common Father. The rite may continue with a Sign of Peace, in which we express the unity we all share in Christ. Then, at Holy Communion, we become one with Christ and with one another. We eat his body broken and drink his blood poured out for the life of the world. The Mass concludes with a blessing and dismissal.

The entire Mass leads up to the distribution of Holy Communion. It is then that extraordinary ministers perform their service. This point of the Mass is dear to the heart of every Catholic.

The Meaning of the Eucharist

The Catholic belief about the Eucharist is at the center of our faith. The New Testament tells us that Jesus gathered his disciples on the night before he died and shared a meal with them. He took, blessed, broke, and gave the bread, saying, "This is my body." Sharing the cup, he said, "This is my blood." All ate and drank, and Jesus commanded them, "Do this in memory of me."[18]

We believe that Jesus intended us to do what he did. We gather to eat and drink a sacred meal, his own Body and Blood.

For us the Mass is both meal and sacrifice. We sit at table with Jesus and dine with him at his Last Supper. We also join the priest in offering this sacrifice to the

> *The cup of blessing that we bless, is it not a participation in the blood of Christ? The bread that we break, is it not a participation in the body of Christ? Because the loaf of bread is one, we, though many, are one body, for we all partake of the one loaf.*
>
> *—1 Corinthians 10:16–17*

praise and glory of God. We call the celebration *Eucharist*, meaning "thanksgiving," or "Mass," indicating that we are sent forth to announce the Good News of salvation. All of these terms represent the joy and challenge of the Eucharist. It brings us life, even as it sends us forth. We greet the coming week confident because of our belief.

We believe that Jesus is Lord, and we confess our faith every time we share Holy Communion. "For as often as you eat this bread and drink the cup, you proclaim the death of the Lord until he comes."[19]

We believe that Christ becomes truly present in the bread and wine consecrated at Mass. Jesus said, "my flesh is true food, and my blood is true drink. Whoever eats my flesh and drinks my blood remains in me."[20]

We believe that Jesus shed his blood for our forgiveness. He said, "This is my blood of the covenant, which will be shed on behalf of many for the forgiveness of sins."[21]

We believe that sharing the Eucharist makes us one. "The cup of blessing that we bless, is it not a participation in the blood of Christ? The bread that we break, is it not a participation in the body of Christ? Because the loaf of bread is one, we, though many, are one body, for we all partake of the one loaf."[22]

The Eucharist truly sits at the center of our faith.

The extraordinary minister, then, supports our faith in all of these matters. The minister inspires our belief in the real presence of Christ, fosters our sense of unity and reconciliation, and helps us profess our belief, our "Amen" to the mystery we receive.

The Qualities of the Extraordinary Minister of Holy Communion

To perform this ministry, the extraordinary minister must be the right kind of person: a baptized Catholic in good standing with the Church. The minister will be a person of faith, who believes in God, follows Christ, and trusts in the Holy Spirit. The minister will have a genuine love for the Eucharist, in order to share the joy

An extraordinary minister must be a baptized Catholic in good standing with the Church.

of Holy Communion with all who partake. The minister will love the Body of Christ in all its forms, and seek to serve the people of God in their times of need.

You have felt God's call to this ministry. You have had to think about the kind of person you are and the meaning of the actions you will perform. You have reflected on your faith, how good God has been to you, and what you have to offer back to the One who made you and blessed you. You have thought about the specific gifts you received from God, and how you might best put them to use for the good of the Church and the world.

Some people feel unworthy of this ministry. They think that they should not be allowed to touch the Body of Christ, to handle the sacred chalice, or to place these elements in the hands of the faithful. These feelings are normal. After all, who is worthy of this great mystery? Every one of us, before we receive Holy Communion, says, "Lord, I am not worthy . . . ."[23] But Christ invites us anyway. Christ makes us worthy by coming to us. No one distributes Holy Communion without having first received it. In the mysterious presence of the risen Jesus, filled with the Holy Spirit, an extraordinary minister is called by God to handle what no one otherwise dares to touch.

Questions for Reflection and Discussion

1. How did it happen that you felt called to serve the Church as an extraordinary minister? Did someone ask you? Did you offer your services?

_____

_____

_____

_____

2. Looking back over your life, what significant steps led you to this ministry? How did you develop your love for the Eucharist? How did you experience the desire for service?

_____

_____

_____

_____

3. Who are your models for this ministry? Who have you seen perform this ministry well? What have you noticed about their lives?

_____

_____

_____

_____

4. What does the Mass mean to you? How is it a part of your spiritual life?

_____

_____

_____

_____

5. In what other ways do you serve the Body of Christ?

_____

_____

_____

_____

NOTES

1. See *The General Instruction of the Roman Missal* (GIRM), 95.

2. See *Code of Canon Law* (CCL), 1247.

3. *Rite of Baptism for Children* (RBC), 62.

4. *Lumen gentium* (LG), 10.

5. Ibid.

6. Ibid.

7. *Catechism of the Catholic Church* (CCC), 1273.

8. *Rite of Confirmation* (RC), 22.

9. LG, 11.

10. Ibid.

11. See GIRM, 95.

12. Ibid. 97.

13. *Fidei custos* (FC), 5.

14. *Immensae caritatis* (IC), 1.

15. Ibid., 1/VI.

16. *Book of Blessings* (BB), 1877–1878.

17. See the Order of Mass in the third edition of *The Roman Missal*.

18. See Luke 22:19–20

19. 1 Corinthians 11:26.

20. John 6:55–56.

21. Matthew 26:28.

22. 1 Corinthians 10:16–17.

23. See the Order of Mass in the third edition of *The Roman Missal*.

Spirituality and Formation of the Extraordinary Minister of Holy Communion

---

I am the bread of life; whoever comes to me will never hunger, and whoever believes in me will never thirst.
—*John 6:35*

Being an extraordinary minister takes more than the few minutes at Mass when you distribute Holy Communion. Good extraordinary ministers take their spiritual growth seriously. As they become comfortable in their service, they feel challenged to do it ever better and more deeply.

Here are some ideas for your spiritual growth. Develop your love for Christ and the Church through the Mass, prayer, and service.

The Mass

As with any Catholic, the single most important spiritual exercise of your life is regular participation at Sunday Mass. Your weekly commitment to the Eucharist demonstrates your faith in the Resurrection, your belief in the real presence of Christ, and your love for your parish community.

When you meet regularly with the same group of worshippers, you get a feel for the community, its wants and needs, its moments of joy and hope. You will develop a repertoire of common hymns of praise, hear the announcements that note forthcoming important events, and follow the preaching from week to week.

You will also come to know names and faces. A good extraordinary minister also will be a good minister of hospitality. Get to know the names of the people with whom you worship. Look at a parish photo directory. Introduce yourself to people before and after Mass. Look for them again at parish events during the week or while shopping for groceries in the neighborhood. Make connections. When you do, you are drawing the community a little bit closer, and you are enhancing the communion of all.

Pay special attention to those in formation for their first Holy Communion. Get to know the catechumens of the parish as well as those baptized Christians preparing for their reception into the full communion of the Catholic Church. The Eucharist will be the climax of their time of formation. Talk to them about their anticipation, and share with them what the Eucharist means to you. Find out which families are preparing children for first Holy Communion this year. Encourage the youth as their big day draws near.

When you serve as an extraordinary minister, be attentive to all your words and actions. Enter the sanctuary at the appointed time. Receive Holy Communion with intention and reverence. Carry the vessels mindful of what they contain. Wait for each person to stand before you. Announce "The Body of Christ" or "The Blood of Christ"[1] with meaning and faith. Wait for the response, and then offer Holy Communion. Afterward, carry the vessels carefully to the appointed place. An extraordinary minister falls into the routine rather quickly, but the pattern should never be thoughtless. Your actions should always be filled with meaning, every step and every word.

When you are not exercising your extraordinary ministry at Mass, still participate with all your skill. Sing the songs, make the responses, assume the postures, listen to the readings, heed the preaching, offer your life to God, and share Holy Communion with your brothers and sisters. Receiving Holy Communion from another minister will school you in the importance of making a sincere presentation to each communicant.

Stay in touch with the Church's liturgical year as well as the civic calendar. The Sacred Paschal Triduum begins on Holy Thursday evening continues through Good Friday and the Easter Vigil, and concludes on Easter Sunday evening. The church services on those days should be of the highest priority for every Catholic, and especially for all who will serve as Communion ministers—clergy and laity alike. The Easter Vigil, the most important Mass of the year, meets in the night to proclaim faith in the Resurrection, opens our ears to the Scriptures that tell of our salvation, welcomes those who are newly baptized, invites us to recommit ourselves to our baptismal promises, and lets us share in the first Eucharist of Easter Time, under the glow of the Paschal candle, in the midst of a community alive with faith in Christ.

Participate at Mass on all Holydays of Obligation and other days of importance. Begin Lent with Ash Wednesday. Give thanks at the Eucharist on Thanksgiving Day. Pray for workers on Labor Day. Observe the seasons of Advent, Christmas Time, Lent, and Easter Time with prayer, decorations, and traditions at home.

Two events on the calendar give special attention to the Eucharist: Evening Mass of the Lord's Supper on Holy Thursday and the Solemnity of the Most Holy Body and Blood of Christ (*Corpus Christi*). Holy Thursday commemorates the night Jesus instituted the Eucharist. This solemnity celebrates the gift of the Eucharist and the devotions that have surrounded it. It is a day of singular importance for Catholics who devote their service to the Church in the distribution of Holy Communion.

Ordinary Time includes a special series of readings devoted to the Eucharist. In Year B of the Sunday Lectionary cycle, the weekly readings of Mark's account of the Gospel are interrupted in late summer by a series from the sixth chapter of John's account. These passages come from the section commonly called the "Bread of Life Discourse,"[2] in which Jesus reveals his most sublime teaching on the Eucharist. Those Gospel accounts are especially worth the additional reflection of the extraordinary minister.

Become aware of the diocesan calendar as well. If possible, attend some of the important celebrations at the cathedral. At the Chrism Mass, for example, priests renew their promises of service to the community. The faithful who attend this liturgy show their support of their priests and pray for the Eucharistic ministry of the diocesan Church.

Some people attend Mass more frequently. Most parishes offer a daily Eucharist, and some extraordinary ministers make it a habit to participate.

Prayer

In addition to participating at Mass, private prayer is essential in the life of any Catholic. It is even more so for the one who serves the Body and Blood of Christ.

You may already have a pattern of daily prayer. Some people follow a routine early in the morning or late at night. Others pray a Rosary sometime during the day. Extraordinary ministers can seek out certain prayers to enhance their ministry.

Praying with Scripture

Try using the Sunday Lectionary as a basis for prayer during the week. Read over the Scriptures slowly and prayerfully. Keep a log of what words or phrases strike you. Read the passages again. Reflect on what

God may be telling you through these readings. Jot down a sentence or so about your meditation. You can repeat this exercise throughout the week, or choose a different reading over a series of days. Don't forget to include the Responsorial Psalm. Praying with the Lectionary will keep you in touch with the liturgical year. It will deepen your appreciation of the most important passages of the Bible. It will open your ears to the Liturgy of the Word at Mass and help you prepare for the Liturgy of the Eucharist.

Read over the Scriptures slowly and prayerfully.

Even if your parish provides a copy of the Scripture readings in the pew, try using your ears, not your eyes, when you go to Mass. Having prepared for Mass by praying over these readings, *listen* to the Word proclaimed, as if you are hearing the voice of God. For, indeed, you are.

Praying in Small Groups

You may pray daily with others as well. If you live with members of your family, gather for prayer before a meal, late at night, or whenever it is convenient. If you make the effort to pray with a smaller community during the week, it will enhance your ability to pray with a larger community on Sunday. Such a prayer can take various forms. The important thing is to pray with others in order to enhance your experience of communal worship.

Liturgy of the Hours

The Liturgy of the Hours is the Church's official prayer to mark the shifting parts of a day. It envisions five prayer times every twenty-four hours. Many people use it just for Morning and Evening Prayer, the two hinges on which the daily liturgy turns. A typical session begins with a hymn and continues with several psalms, which lead to a short reading from Scripture. The liturgy concludes with a series of petitions and prayers, including the Lord's Prayer. The Liturgy of the Hours relies on the Church's daily calendar. It honors the saints and festivals of the year. It provides a routine of prayer steeped in the psalms, the Bible, and the liturgical calendar. It can be used privately or in groups. Familiarity with the Liturgy of the Hours will broaden your appreciation of the seasons of the liturgical year as we progress through them at Sunday Mass.

Eucharistic Devotions

Because your ministry is tied to the Eucharist, you also may benefit from Eucharistic devotions. If possible, pray before the Blessed Sacrament at church. Take time before or after Mass, or whenever the church is open, to pray before the tabernacle. Participate in adoration and benediction of the exposed Blessed Sacrament when available, as well as Eucharistic processions.

Participate in adoration and benediction of the exposed Blessed Sacrament when available, as well as Eucharistic processions.

Workshops and Retreats

Watch for workshops that explain more about the Eucharist and the liturgy of the Church. Taking a day or more to educate yourself can refresh your spiritual life and increase your understanding of the ministry you provide.

Make a retreat each year. Some parishes offer a day of renewal for their liturgical ministers, but there also may be a monastery, convent, or house of prayer nearby where you can spend longer periods of time alone, with your family, or with other ministers.

Sacrament of Reconciliation

Make use of the Sacrament of Reconciliation. All extraordinary ministers should be persons of integrity whose way of life inspires others to live for Christ. As you become aware of sin, as you see the patterns of behavior that need to be changed, bring your contrition to confession and experience the mercy of God. Don't be satisfied with bad habits or dismissive of temptation's power. Jesus shed his blood for the forgiveness of sins. We become ambassadors of reconciliation as we experience this sacrament and extend God's mercy to others. If extraordinary ministers are forgiven and forgiving, it will show in their daily life and in their participation at the Mass.

For deeper growth, use the same confessor again and again, someone who can come to know you and help you overcome your most persistent faults. That confessor might serve as a spiritual advisor to help you throughout your life. Or you may choose another spiritual director, male or female, with whom you share your inner thoughts, struggles, and hopes.

Spiritual Reading

Develop a habit of spiritual reading. Subscribe to periodicals about the liturgy or prayer. Look for books about the Mass, about saints devoted to the Eucharist, or about service given to others. Read how someone else has put together a spiritual life, and receive advice for your own. You can find some materials on the Internet, but a book, magazine, or e-book might allow you to go someplace away from your normal work station to meditate on the will of God.

Helpful Prayers

You also may keep a file of some of your favorite prayers. Here are two you may want to know about.

After the priest or deacon has purified the vessels after Holy Communion, you may be asked to clean these vessels with soap and water. You might want to say the prayer that *The Roman Missal* recommends when the priest performs the duty of cleaning the vessels.

What has passed our lips as food, O Lord,
may we possess in purity of heart,
that what has been given to us in time
may be our healing for eternity.

This beloved prayer, *Pange Lingua,* was composed by St. Thomas Aquinas in the thirteenth century.

Hail our Savior's glorious Body,
*   which his Virgin Mother bore;*
hail the Blood which, shed for sinners,
*   did a broken world restore;*
hail the sacrament most holy,
*   flesh and Blood of Christ adore!*

Come adore this wondrous presence;
*   bow to Christ, the source of grace!*
Here is kept the ancient promise
*   of God's earthly dwelling-place!*
Sight is blind before God's glory,
*   faith alone may see his face!*

Service

You will grow in your ministry if you serve the Body of Christ outside of the liturgy as well. Look for opportunities to feed the hungry and give drink to the thirsty, and to wash the feet of others, as Jesus did.

If there is a soup kitchen in your area, give some time to help out with preparing or serving the meal. Visit with the people who come and give them a friendly welcome. You could offer the same kind of service at a nearby nursing home.

When your parish prepares a meal for some event, bring food. Or help with the cleanup. It's often hard to find someone willing and stay to the end and make sure the place is ready to use again the next day.

Become active in organizations that provide food for the hungry and drinking water for those without it. Write your senators and representatives, asking them to allocate sufficient funds in the budget to make hunger history. Assist the relief efforts for those deprived of food and water due to natural disasters around the world.

Even at home, whenever you help in the kitchen, let it be a form of prayer that prepares you for the Eucharistic meal. Provide food and drink for your family. Host a meal for friends. Bake your own bread, and get a sense of what it means when we say that Jesus is the bread of life or that we gather at church for the breaking of the bread.

You can grow spiritually in many ways, especially through prayer and service. Perform the activities that will deepen your understanding of what you do when you give the Body and Blood of Christ to those who hunger and thirst for it.

Questions for Reflection and Discussion

1. What are my primary spiritual exercises these days? Sunday Mass? Daily prayer?

_____

_____

_____

_____

_____

2. How did I develop these? What made them important to me?

_____

_____

_____

_____

_____

3. As I look to the future, what prayer would I like to use to enhance my ministry?

_____

_____

_____

_____

4. What kinds of service am I doing right now that deepen my appreciation for the Body of Christ?

_____

_____

_____

_____

5. How is a meal at home like the meal at Mass? Who performs different "ministries"? What "word" is shared? What prayers are said?

_____

_____

_____

_____

NOTES

1. See the Order of Mass in the third edition of *The Roman Missal.*

2. See John 6:22–59.

Serving as an Extraordinary Minister of Holy Communion

*May the saving mysteries they distribute /
lead them to the joys of eternal life.*

—Book of Blessings, 1878

You have felt God's call to serve the Church as an extraordinary minister of Holy Communion. This role is extremely important for the celebration of the Eucharist. It is a ministry that will require you to grow in confidence and reverence in the way you handle the Blessed Sacrament, as well as in kindness, charity, and humility towards your brothers and sisters in the community of faith. You will need to learn and keep learning. As the bishops of the United States of America have taught, extraordinary ministers "should receive sufficient spiritual, theological, and practical preparation to fulfill their role with knowledge and reverence."[1] This resource will help supplement your preparation and training from your parish or diocese.

Extraordinary ministers of Holy Communion are deputed to assist the priest and deacon with distributing Holy Communion during Mass, to bring Holy Communion to the sick and the homebound, and to give Viaticum to the dying. While not all extraordinary ministers who serve at Mass bring Holy Communion to the sick, homebound, and the dying, and vice versa, the roles are closely interconnected.[2] This chapter will walk you through the basics of what you need to know to be effective — and happy — in this important ministry of service.

The role of the extraordinary minister is extremely important for the celebration of the Eucharist.

Serving at Mass

Being Prepared

It is normal, in fact, expected, for cantors, choir members, instrumentalists, lectors and readers to do extensive preparation for their Sunday ministry. They review their music and practice it, they read their reading over and over again, they look up unfamiliar names, words, or confusing passages and check the context in the Bible. For extraordinary ministers of Holy Communion, there's little to rehearse, but there is much to prepare for.[3]

Preparing by Prayer

Administering Holy Communion to your brothers and sisters in the Body of Christ is the best possible Communion meditation. But serving in this ministry means the Communion Rite is a busy time for you: you have to stay focused, attentive, and on your feet. It can sometimes feel like you were too busy to pray! So it is especially important that you take time for prayer before Mass. Reflect on the Scriptures. Ponder the Prayer over the Offerings and the Prayer after Communion, which almost always relate in a special way to this ministry. Pray before the Blessed Sacrament. Your manner of life and your habits of prayer should always be in keeping with the importance of the ministry to which you have been called.

An extraordinary minister must be a person of prayer.

Scheduling

Whether your parish is large or small, your community depends on you to know when you are scheduled to serve, and to be there on time. More and more parishes are using scheduling software to create the schedule for your ministry and to keep it up-to-date. Some of these programs allow you to check your schedule online, request substitutes by e-mail, and even add events to your personal calendar with the click of a mouse! Whether your system is high-tech or low-tech, it's very important to be there when you are scheduled, or to arrange for a substitute when you are not. Know whom you should contact if there is a last-minute illness or emergency. You are being entrusted with great things: be responsible in the little things, too.

Most parishes assign extraordinary ministers to "stations" or places for distribution ahead of time. Know what and where your station is ahead of time. Check in with the coordinator of your ministry as sometimes the station may need to be adjusted or rearranged. When this happens, go with the flow!

The very title of our ministry—extraordinary minister of Holy Communion—reminds us that we are not the "ordinary" ministers, the bishop, priest, or deacon. We exercise our ministry only when sufficient ordinary ministers are not available. Be patient if the presence of an additional priest or of a deacon means that you are not needed to serve at a particular Mass, even if you have been scheduled. This happens rarely, but it does occasionally happen. Accept it as part of being "extraordinary"!

Clothing and Vesture

In the United States, extraordinary ministers of Holy Communion and other liturgical ministers may wear an alb. The alb, a baptismal garment, adds a dignified simplicity to the liturgy and serves as a reminder to extraordinary ministers and to the assembly that all the service we undertake for the Church is rooted in our Baptism. While the alb is an option, in many places extraordinary ministers carry out their ministry in their street clothes, and that can be an added challenge. Dress simply, modestly, and appropriately. You don't need to wear your Easter best every Sunday of the year, but leave your jeans, shorts, sneakers, tank tops, and T-shirts with slogans, including religious, of any kind at home. Some parishes have a written policy indicating appropriate dress for those involved in this ministry. Know what the norms are in your parish and abide by them carefully. They are there both for you and for others, to ensure that you can carry out your ministry, and people can receive Holy Communion, with dignity and without distraction.

During Mass

While the most active part of your ministry begins with the Communion Rite, you should model "full, conscious, and active participation"[4] throughout the Mass. Arrive on time. Be attentive during Mass. If there is a song sheet or worship aid, use it. If directed to the hymnal, open it. Stand, kneel, and sit as appropriate. During the Sign of Peace, greet those in your immediate vicinity with joy and warmth. People will begin to recognize you as someone with an important responsibility in the parish, and whether you realize it or not, they will look to you for an example of how to participate fully, consciously, and actively in the Mass.[5]

Approaching the Altar

After the priest has received Holy Communion, the extraordinary ministers move towards the altar so that they can receive Holy Communion before they begin to distribute either the Precious Body or Precious Blood. Extraordinary ministers "should not approach the altar before the Priest has received Communion. . . ."[6]

A question that communities continue to grapple with is what exactly does the phrase "approach the altar" mean? Does this mean extraordinary ministers can be in the sanctuary—but not at the altar—prior to the priest celebrant's reception of Holy Communion? The norms of your diocesan bishop (or, in their absence, the directives given by the pastor of your parish) will tell you what to do.[7]

In a small congregation, it will be relatively easy for two or three extraordinary ministers to approach the altar at the proper time, receive Holy Communion, and then be handed the vessels they need. But in larger congregations, where more extraordinary ministers are involved, things can get complicated and careful preparation will be needed to ensure that the reception of Holy Communion not be unnecessarily delayed. Understand and follow the practices set in place by your parish leadership.

Extraordinary ministers should not approach the altar until the priest has received Holy Communion.

When should extraordinary ministers receive Holy Communion themselves? When we are serving people in our homes—at a festive meal like Thanksgiving or Christmas, for example—we consider it good hospitality to serve others, and then serve ourselves. But that is not the case in the celebration of the Eucharist. We are not the hosts, but guests at the table of the Lord. It is always Christ who is serving and all of us who are being served. Therefore, "[t]he practice of extraordinary ministers of Holy Communion waiting to receive Holy Communion until after the distribution of Holy Communion is not in accord with liturgical law."[8] We cannot give what we have not yet received.[9]

Keeping Good Order

When the lay ministers approach the altar, they may divide into two groups, depending on whether they are distributing the Body of Christ or the Precious Blood. The host ministers might go to the right, the chalice ministers to the left, or they could be in two separate rows. The priest can begin by giving the host to each of the ministers. Then he can return to the altar and distribute the chalices and purificators to the ministers of the Precious Blood. Each of these ministers can receive from their chalice before moving with it to their station. If no deacon is present, at least one extraordinary minister should be designated to present the Blood of Christ to the host ministers before they are handed their bowls or patens and move to their own stations in the sanctuary.

If a deacon is present, distribution of Holy Communion to the extraordinary ministers can be more streamlined. The priest can give the Body of Christ to each minister, while the deacon follows and gives each of them Holy Communion from the chalice. Then both priest and deacon can return to the altar to distribute the vessels to the extraordinary ministers.

Every church building and every sanctuary is slightly different, so there is no "right way" to arrange the extraordinary ministers. Every parish community will need to find its own system that allows the extraordinary ministers to receive Holy Communion reverently and smoothly, without awkwardness or undue delay. Oftentimes, diocesan norms or parish practice will determine where you should stand in the sanctuary in order to receive Holy Communion. In order to avoid any confusion of liturgical roles during the celebration of the Eucharistic liturgy, extraordinary ministers may not stand in the traditional positions of concelebrating priests (that is standing alongside or in rows behind the priest at the altar).

Receiving Holy Communion

Everything you do during Mass matters. Receive Holy Communion in such a way that any Catholic who watches you can imitate what you do. Receive with reverence, dignity, and attention. It is your choice whether to receive the host on the tongue or in the hand.[10] If you receive on the tongue, say "Amen," then open your mouth and extend your tongue just slightly, to make it easy for the minister to give you Holy Communion without touching your mouth. If you receive in the hand, remember the words of St. Cyril of Jerusalem: "When you approach, take care not to do so with your hand stretched out and your fingers open or apart, but rather place your left hand as a throne beneath your right, as befits one who is about to receive the King. Then receive him, taking care that nothing is lost."[11] Handle the chalice with care, receiving it from the minister with both hands, taking just a small amount, not a large mouthful, and handing it back to the minister with equal reverence. It is customary in the United States to bow your head before receiving the Body and Blood of Christ.

> *When you approach, take care not to do so with your hand stretched out and your fingers open or apart, but rather place your left hand as a throne beneath your right, as befits one who is about to recieve the King. Then receive him, taking care that nothing is lost: "This is my blood of the covenant, which will be shed on behalf of many for the forgiveness of sins."*
>
> —*St. Cyril of Jerusalem*

Finding your Station

Everyone who is distributing Holy Communion should have a clear understanding of where his or her assigned station will be. In general, host ministers stand at the head of the center aisles. In especially large churches, host ministers may also be stationed at the crossing (halfway down the nave), or at the head of side aisles or transept seating sections.

The ministers holding the chalices are always stationed in relation to the host ministers. Whenever Holy Communion is given under both kinds, there should be at least one—or, ideally, two—chalices for each paten or ciborium: "For Communion from the chalice, it is desirable that there be generally two ministers of the Precious Blood for each minister of the Body of Christ, lest the liturgical celebration be unduly prolonged."[12] When this is not possible, a single minister of the chalice should watch carefully to ensure that the line does not become too long. If the line stretches to the point that the host minister is impeded from distributing Holy Communion, the chalice minister can take a step or two farther away from the host minister's position, if possible, to provide some additional room.

After you receive the chalice or the vessel for hosts, move to your station (in some places, ministers wait until all have received their vessels to move to their stations; in other places, they move one after the other,

After you receive the chalice or the vessel for hosts, move to your station to distribute Holy Communion.

as each receives the vessel. There is no "right" way—just follow the practice in your community). Most often, you will be carrying the hosts in an uncovered bowl or ciborium. Hold the vessel securely with one hand, and gently cover it with the other as you move to your station. If you are giving Holy Communion from the chalice, hold the chalice securely with one hand; you can place the purificator over the chalice and rest your other hand on top of it.

When accidents happen, it is usually when ministers are not sure where they are going. Be sure you know your station, so that when you are moving to it you can concentrate on carrying the Blessed Sacrament with care and reverence.

Distributing Holy Communion

As you begin to distribute Holy Communion, focus on each communicant as if he or she were the only person in line. Make eye contact. Elevate the host slightly, between your thumb and first finger, and say in a distinct, but not loud voice, "The Body of Christ."[13] The communicant bows and responds, "Amen." Then place the host in the outstretched hands or on the tongue of the communicant.[14]

When presenting the chalice, extend and elevate the chalice slightly as the communicant approaches, with the words, "The Blood of Christ." The communicant bows and says "Amen" and takes the chalice from your hands to receive Communion, then hands the chalice back to you. You do not need to hold on to the chalice the entire time. Carefully wipe the rim of the chalice, both inside and outside, where the communicant's lips touched it. Turn the chalice slightly—about a quarter-turn—so that the next communicant's lips will touch a different section of the rim.

Many extraordinary ministers find it helpful to hold the chalice by the stem with their dominant hand while holding the purificator with their other hand. In this way, the communicant can choose either to grasp the bowl of the chalice with both hands, or to receive the chalice by placing one hand on the chalice's bowl and the other below the base. Because each communicant's way of receiving will be different, it does take some practice to give and receive the chalice both simply and reverently. Unfold the purificator. After you have handed the chalice to the communicant following his or her "Amen," you will have a moment to find a fresh place on the purificator to wipe the rim of the chalice.

Hold the chalice by the stem, using your dominant hand, and hold the purificator in your other hand.

In general, the ciborium or the chalice should be held comfortably at chest height, neither too high nor too low. Adjust the height to accommodate the height or physical dexterity of the communicant. For example, some children and elderly persons may be unsteady when receiving. Be attentive to the needs of each communicant as you distribute Holy Communion.

Take time to handle the sacred vessels before Mass, so that you can get comfortable with the shape and weight of the chalice, paten, or ciborium, and be able to handle them more reverently and confidently during Mass. Even if you have been involved in the ministry for a long time, your parish may use different vessels in different liturgical seasons. The first time you encounter a new paten, chalice, or ciborium should not be during the Mass.

Communicants, too, have some choices in how they receive. In receiving the host, they may choose to receive in the hand or on the tongue. While reception in the hand is the more ancient practice, receiving on the tongue is also part of a long and venerable tradition, and it is the prerogative of the communicant to decide how he or she will receive Holy Communion.[15] In the United States, the norm is to receive Holy Communion standing,[16] but if someone should kneel to receive, give them Holy Communion in the same reverent manner. Church documents make it clear that none of the faithful should be denied Holy Communion solely on the grounds that the person wishes to receive the Eucharist kneeling or standing.[17]

Whether they receive in the hand or on the tongue, each communicant is to receive, not take the host from the communion minister.[18] The way you distribute Holy Communion—by gently placing the Body of Christ into the "throned" hands of a communicant or gently upon their tongue—will help encourage the communicant to receive properly and reverently. When you speak the words "The Body of Christ" clearly and distinctly, you may also encourage the communicant to reply with a stronger, more deliberate "Amen."

Communicants can choose to receive on the tongue or in the hand.

Those who receive the host in the hand should immediately consume the Body of Christ. In some places, it is the custom to take a step to the side and receive, but they should not move farther than that while carrying the Eucharistic species in their hands. Extraordinary ministers of Holy Communion share with the priest the responsibility to ensure that the Eucharistic species is cared for at every moment and properly and reverently consumed at Communion time. If you notice a communicant moving away with the host, or if someone approaches the chalice while still holding the host in their hand, gently ask them to consume the host immediately.[19]

"It is the choice of the communicant, not the minister, to receive from the chalice."[20] Some may choose not to receive from the chalice for health or other reasons. In the same way, those with gluten intolerance or celiac disease may choose not to receive the host if low-gluten hosts are not offered at the Mass, but simply to receive from the chalice. These are choices to be made by the communicant.[21]

Within the United States, the norms direct that the communicant is to bow his or her head before the sacrament as gesture of reverence.

Things to remember:

> ✠ When receiving Holy Communion, the communicant bows his or her head before the Sacrament as a gesture of reverence and receives the Body of the Lord from the minister.
>
> —*General Instruction of the Roman Missal, 160*

- Look each communicant in the eye, recognizing in them the Body of Christ even as you give them his Body and Blood in Holy Communion.

- Remember that it is not permitted to change the formulas for the giving of Holy Communion[22]: "The Body of Christ." "The Blood of Christ." This would include adding personal names, such as, "Paul, the Body of Christ," or "The Body of Christ, Mary." While this may seem like a warm and friendly way to encounter someone you know, it can actually create divisions. Chances are, you won't know everyone who is present, you'll end up creating two categories: friends and strangers.

- Be yourself. Let your joy shine through in the way you distribute Holy Communion. Smile!

- Carry and hold the vessels with care and reverence, showing by your actions that this is no ordinary food and drink.

- Use the entire purificator. Open it and wipe the rim of the chalice with a clean spot on the purificator each time. You have a moment to turn the purificator and find a clean spot as each person receives from the chalice.

- Elevate the host and chalice slightly, based on the height of the person who receives. Hold it higher for a tall person, lower for a child or shorter adult.

- Stay calm and focused. If you are running out of hosts, keep your focus on the next person in line until you actually run out; then quietly go to the tabernacle, the sacristan, or the master of ceremonies, according to the practice in your community. If someone seems confused about how to receive Holy Communion or takes what you consider to be too much Precious Blood, be sure not to let your face or body language express your disapproval.

- Remember that the Communion procession is a sacred moment. It is not the place for arguments or struggles; nor is it the place for catechesis on who can receive Holy Communion or how to do it. If an issue arises, discuss it with the priest or your ministry coordinator after Mass.

Special Needs

Make sure you are aware of those with special needs.

Be aware of those who may not be able to join the Communion procession. The musicians are usually the last to come forward for Holy Communion, because they are busy leading the music during the Communion procession. Wait for the cantor, organist, choir, or instrumentalists before returning the sacred vessels to the altar or credence table. If Communion is given under both kinds, be sure that the chalice is available to them as well as the host.

Be aware also of those who are not able to come forward to receive Holy Communion—the elderly or people with other physical limitations. Sometimes, those who are unable to come forward sit in a designated section of the church so that the priest, deacon, or extraordinary minister can bring them Holy Communion either at the beginning or at the end of the Communion procession. At other times, they will be in the midst of the assembly and an usher or family member may alert you to their presence.

Returning the Vessels

When you finish distributing Holy Communion, the patens or ciboria are usually returned to the altar, where the priest or deacon combines the fragments into the ciborium and returns them to the tabernacle. The chalices, meanwhile, are usually taken either to the altar or to the credence table.[23] It is customary to consume what is left in your chalice— "When there are extraordinary ministers of Holy Communion, they may consume what remains of the Precious Blood from their chalice of distribution with permission of the Diocesan Bishop."[24] Know what the guidelines are in your own diocese. If for health reasons you are unable to consume what is left, or if there is too much for you to consume by yourself, ask for help.

Returning to Your Seat

In some communities, extraordinary ministers return to their seats individually after taking the vessels to the altar or a side table. Others parishes have the extraordinary ministers return from the sanctuary or altar area as a group. Be sure to know your parish practice.

After Mass

The purification of the sacred vessels is a task reserved to a priest, deacon, or instituted acolyte. After returning all the remaining hosts to the tabernacle, and consuming the remaining Precious Blood, the priest or deacon purifies the vessels by rinsing them in a small amount of water, which he then consumes, and wiping them with a purificator. After this task is completed, the vessels may be washed with soap and water in the usual manner.[25] In many parishes, the extraordinary ministers of Holy Communion are expected to help with this task. If that is the case in your parish, then make yourself available in the sacristy after Mass to assist.

Prayer

Prayer after Mass is as important as prayer before Mass. Include a special prayer for all those to whom you were privileged to give Holy Communion this day, and for all those who are unable to receive Holy Communion.

Communion outside of Mass

The Order for the Commissioning of Extraordinary Ministers of Holy Communion states that "our brothers and sisters . . . are to be entrusted with administering the eucharist, with taking communion to the sick, and with giving it as viaticum to the dying."[26] We are commissioned not simply to serve during the Mass, but to extend Christ's presence beyond the walls of the church by bringing the sacramental presence of Christ to those who cannot join the parish for worship, and especially to the sick.

Ritual Texts for Lay Ministers

Sunday Celebrations in the Absence of a Priest

Depending on the practice in your diocese and parish, in the absence of a priest for the Saturday night Vigil Masses or Sunday Masses you may be called upon to assist or even to preside at what is commonly called a "Communion service"—that is, at the Rite of Distributing Holy Communion Outside Mass. The ritual text *Sunday Celebrations in the Absence of a Priest* includes two formats for this service. One centers on the proclamation of the Word of God. It begins with a greeting, a Penitential Act as at Mass, and then continues with the Liturgy of the Word. This may include all the Mass readings, or simply a short passage focused on the Eucharist. The service continues with the Universal Prayer, and then moves to the Communion Rite, which is similar to the Mass, with the Lord's Prayer, Sign of Peace, and reception of Holy Communion. The service ends with a prayer, and, when a deacon presides, with a blessing and dismissal. The other format incorporates the celebration of the Office of Morning Prayer or Evening Prayer from the Liturgy of the Hours, and includes the singing of a hymn, the recitation of the psalms and canticles from the office, and intercessions. After the Gospel Canticle (the Canticle of Zechariah at Morning Prayer, the Canticle of Mary at Evening Prayer) the Communion Rite begins. It should be noted that both forms are intended for Sundays, not for weekdays. Know and observe the norms in your diocese and parish.

Pastoral Care of the Sick

When giving Communion in a nursing home, hospital, or to the home-bound, one of two rites in the *Pastoral Care of the Sick: Rites of Anointing and Viaticum* is used.[27] The first, called "Communion in Ordinary Circumstances," closely resembles the rite described above—a simple Liturgy of the Word followed by a Communion Rite, but with texts that focus on healing, strength, and courage for the sick. It is ideal when leading a Communion service for a group of people in a nursing home or hospital. The second, called "Communion in a Hospital or Institution," is much simpler and is a good choice for bringing Communion to an individual, whether at home or in the hospital. It includes a brief anti-phon (which can be said once at the beginning of the entire visit when you are bringing Communion to several different rooms) and can include a Scripture passage, "if there is time and it seems desirable."[28] Then it moves immediately to the Lord's Prayer and the giving and receiving of Holy Communion, and concludes with a simple prayer of thanksgiving.

Ministry to the homebound and the sick is a special calling. It requires patience and flexibility. Bring each person the love and care of the parish community as you bring them Holy Communion. Work on your "bedside manner." Take time before the rite for giving Holy Communion to talk, however briefly, about how the person is doing, and what concerns are uppermost for him or her at the moment. Be sure to acknowledge the family members and friends who may be present, and include them in the conversation and prayer depending on their comfort level. When you and the sick person are both ready, continue with the Communion Rite. At the end of the rite, don't slip back into chit-chat, but end the visit so that the person has time to reflect and pray after receiving Holy Communion.

In hospitals, of course, it will probably not be possible to do much set-up before leading the service. Whenever possible, spread out a cor-poral and place the pyx on it, light candles, and have a small crucifix nearby. All the rites for giving Holy Communion outside of Mass call for a few moments of adoration after the pyx containing the Blessed Sacrament is placed on the table.

When you are bringing Holy Communion to a homebound person on a regular basis, you might be able to establish a "sacred space" that is used week after week. The homebound person may wish to arrange this space themselves, with candles to light, a crucifix, and images of favorite saints.

Note that all of these rites will involve Holy Communion under one kind only, because the Precious Blood is not reserved after Mass.

Handling the Unexpected

Knowing how to handle the Blessed Sacrament and how to distribute Holy Communion to God's people is important. Almost as important is knowing how to handle the unexpected, because the unexpected always happens.

If the Body of Christ Is Dropped

If a host, or part of a host, falls to the floor, simply bend down and pick it up immediately and reverently.[29] The host should be kept separate and consumed after Holy Communion. You might hold the dropped host in the palm of the hand that you are using to hold the paten or ciborium, until you are free to give it to the priest or sacristan following the distribution of Holy Communion.

If, on the other hand, the host is seriously soiled—that is, if it has fallen from someone's mouth, or if it has fallen on a wet or very dirty floor—it is not consumed following Mass, but reverently disposed of by being placed in a vessel of water following Mass, where it can dissolve until it can be poured down the sacrarium.[30] The priest, deacon, or sacristan in your community will be able to direct the proper way of disposing of a consecrated host or fragment of a host that cannot be consumed by a minister following Mass.

The situation more often arises when Holy Communion is given in nursing homes and hospitals, and when the communicant is not able to swallow all or part of the host. In these cases, the soiled host or fragment should be placed in a clean plastic bag or wrapped in a clean handkerchief, or placed back in the pyx, and returned to the parish for proper disposal, as described above.

Extraordinary ministers of Holy Communion, whether distributing Holy Communion during Mass or in another setting, should note that these are the only proper ways of disposing of a consecrated host.

If the Precious Blood Is Spilled

If a drop falls from the chalice, immediately use your purificator or corporal to wipe it up. Usually such spills are quite small and you can use a small portion of your purificator to clean it up, and then continue using the same purificator to wipe the chalice as you distribute Holy Communion. In the case of a larger spill, you may need to ask the sacristan for a fresh purificator before you can continue distributing Holy Communion. Take your time in cleaning up when the Precious Blood is spilled.

Following Holy Communion or after Mass, the place where the Precious Blood was spilled should be wiped down with a damp cloth, which is then rinsed in the sacrarium like other altar linens.[31] This is usually not the responsibility of the individual extraordinary ministers, but of the sacristan. Know whom to alert in your parish.

If the communicant spills the Precious Blood on himself or herself, hand them the purificator, and gently encourage them to wipe their chin or garment.[32]

Requests for Communion by Intinction

Sometimes communicants may approach you to receive by intinction, which is an acceptable form of receiving Holy Communion in the Roman Catholic Church, though it is not often used in the Catholic Churches of the United States. "Intinction" means that the consecrated host is dipped into the chalice, and the priest then administers Holy Communion under both forms at the same time, using the words "The Body and Blood of Christ" and placing the intincted host directly on the tongue, never in the hand. Notice that it is never permitted for the communicant to dip the host into the chalice and receive for himself or herself.

The challenge with intinction is that even though it is a legitimate way to receive in the Church, only a bishop or a priest—not even a deacon!—may give Holy Communion in this way.[33] That puts an extraordinary minister in an awkward position. The best practice when someone approaches holding the host is to cover the chalice with the purificator, and say gently, "please consume your host and then you can receive from the chalice." If the communicant requests intinction, you can simply say "I'm not permitted to give you Communion by intinction, but after you receive your host I can give Communion from the chalice." If you meet with great hardship after your invitation for consuming the host first— remember, the Communion line is not the place for catechesis, but, as a lay minister, you should be respectful to the Church's theology, behavior, and ritual. Try to mentally note that person, so that following Mass, you can speak with the priest, ministry coordinator, or other proper staff person can speak to them about the proper ways of receiving Holy Communion.

All extraordinary ministers should be watchful during the Communion procession to make sure that each communicant consumes the host before returning to his or her place in the church. It doesn't happen often, but occasionally someone will walk back to their place holding the host. If someone moves away with the host still in hand, simply walk over to them and quietly ask them to consume the host right away. Often, the minister of the Precious Blood is in a better position to see a potential problem than the minister with the Body of Christ, but all extraordinary ministers should be watchful and attentive throughout the Communion Rite.

Doubts about Eligibility to Receive Holy Communion

While Christ wishes to feed everyone with his Body and Blood, not everyone is ready to receive him. Some who may join the community for prayer are not yet baptized or not Catholic. It is true that on some occasions non-Catholic Christians may be admitted to Holy Communion; these circumstances are very rare and must be arranged with the priest in accordance with canon law. While we all pray for the unity of Christians, genuine ecumenism acknowledges the divisions that exist between churches—to receive Holy Communion where there is not yet unity is, quite simply, false ecumenism.

Sometimes Catholics are impeded from receiving Holy Communion, most often because they are divorced and remarried. In recent years there have also been a number of unfortunate and high-profile cases of people who have been denied Holy Communion when they presented themselves in line, generally because of their political stance or another reason. Remember, the Church makes it easy for extraordinary ministers: our task is simply to give Holy Communion, never to withhold it unless specifically directed by the bishop or priest. It is that simple. If you have questions or concerns about someone who has come forward for Communion, speak to the priest after Mass.

As an extraordinary minister, you will encounter situations in which you are simply not sure whether the person should receive or not. Someone may come forward without extending their hands, opening their mouth, or otherwise indicating that they wish to receive. In these cases, you can simply ask, "are you Catholic and wish to receive?" which will usually prompt the person to assume the correct posture. Sometimes, young children will come forward who seem to you either too young or unprepared for Communion. In these cases, you can simply ask the adult who brought them, "does he or she receive Communion?" If the child does receive, the adult will usually help the child assume the proper posture for reception of Holy Communion.

Keeping Things in Perspective

When something goes wrong—when you spill from the chalice, when you drop a host, when you're not sure you did the right thing—don't agonize or blame yourself or others; pray. A good prayer for extraordinary ministers of Holy Communion is the Divine Praises, the litany that is usually said at Benediction of the Blessed Sacrament, and that originated as a way to respond positively when what we regard as holy and precious is profaned. Most often, the problems that arise during Mass are simply mistakes, not profanations. But blessing God is always good!

Blessed be God.
Blessed be his holy name.
Blessed be Jesus Christ, true God and true man.
Blessed be the name of Jesus.
Blessed be his most Sacred Heart.
Blessed be his most precious Blood.
Blessed be Jesus in the most holy sacrament of the Altar.
Blessed be the Holy Spirit, the paraclete.
Blessed be the great Mother of God, Mary most holy.
Blessed be her holy and Immaculate Conception.
Blessed be her glorious Assumption.
Blessed be the name of Mary, Virgin and Mother.
Blessed be Saint Joseph, her most chaste spouse.
Blessed be God in his angels and in his saints.

Additional Responsibilities

Further Formation

Even after you have completed your training and have begun your service as an extraordinary minister, you need to keep growing spiritually to serve well. Take advantage of days of recollection and retreats. Spend

"Christ is truly present among us in the Eucharist" (Pope Benedict XVI).

time in Eucharistic adoration. Take part in benediction and Eucharistic processions. Grow closer to the Lord. Look at the suggestions in "Spirituality and Formation of the Extraordinary Minister of Holy Communion" on page 19. The resource section on page 63 lists books that will help you continue to grow in understanding of the mystery you are privileged to share.

In the words of Pope Benedict XVI, in his homily closing the 2005 Italian Eucharistic Congress,

Christ is truly present among us in the Eucharist. His presence is not static. It is a dynamic presence that grasps us, to make us his own, to make us assimilate him. Christ draws us to him, he makes us come out of ourselves to make us all one with him. In this way he also integrates us in the communities of brothers and sisters, and communion with the Lord is always also communion with our brothers and sisters. And we see the beauty of this communion that the Blessed Eucharist gives us.[34]

Questions for Discussion and Reflection

1. What excites you about serving as an extraordinary minister of Holy Communion? What intimidates you?

_____

_____

_____

_____

_____

2. Can you think of a time when the minister (whether "ordinary" or "extraordinary") made a difference, negative or positive, in the holy moment of receiving Communion?

_____

_____

_____

_____

_____

3. What are the most important qualities for an extraordinary minister to have? What are the most important things for an extraordinary minister to know?

_____

_____

_____

_____

_____

NOTES

1. *Norms for the Distribution and Reception of Holy Communion under Both Kinds in the Dioceses of the United States of America* (NDRHC), 28.

2. See GIRM, 100, 164, 284; NDRHC, 25, 28; *Book of Blessings* (BB), 1875.

3. See the spirituality chapter in this book on page 19 for additional ways to prepare for your ministry.

4. *Constitution on the Sacred Liturgy* (CSL), 14.

5. Ibid.

6. See *The General Instruction of the Roman Missal* 43, 162; NDRHC, 38.

7. The Bishops' Committee on Divine Worship has responded to a concern about not unduly delaying the Mass when a large number of extraordinary ministers are utilized. "The Extraordinary Ministers of Holy Communion approach the altar as the priest receives Communion" (October 2002, XXXVIII:99). Recognizing that large numbers (eight, for example, in the BCDW text noted) of extraordinary ministers are often desired, the bishop's committee foresees the simultaneous movement of the extraordinary ministers to the altar "as" the celebrant is receiving Holy Communion—not after, so that there is less delay in receiving Holy Communion. In formulating your instructions, your parish leadership will use common sense.

8. NDRHC, 39.

9. The priest (or deacon) hands the sacred vessels to the extraordinary minister for their reception of Holy Communion and then for distribution to the faithful. This is because we are guests at this banquet, not hosts; what we give is not something of our own, but simply what we have been given by Christ. See GIRM, 162; NDRHC, 38, 40.

10. Extraordinary ministers may receive either on the tongue or in the hand but may never "receive Holy Communion in the manner of a concelebrating Priest" (NDRHC, 39; GIRM, 284; NDRHC, 50), that is, holding the host in the hand during the Lamb of God, and receiving together with the celebrant following the "Lord, I am not worthy. . . ." An extraordinary minister may also never self-communicate at Mass, which means that it is not permissible for a lay person to pick up the chalice or host for themselves and receive from it.

11. Quoted in NDRHC, 41.

12. NDRHC, 30.

13. When giving Holy Communion, it is not permitted to modify or change "The Body of Christ" and "The Blood of Christ" (see the *Constitution on the Sacred Liturgy* (CSL) which states, "no other person, not even if he is a priest, may, on his own, add, remove, or change anything in the liturgy" [CSL, 22; see also GIRM, 24).

14. If a person chooses to receive on the tongue take care that your fingers do not touch the tongue of the communicant. It's the communicant's choice—not the decision of the Communion minister—whether to receive on the tongue or, in areas, where the Bishop's Conference has approved and received permission by the Holy See, in the hand (See RS, 92, 94).

15. NDRHC, 41.

16. GIRM, 160 states: "The norm established for the Dioceses of the United States of America is that Holy Communion is to be received standing, unless an individual member of the faithful wishes to receive Communion while kneeling. . . . When receiving Holy Communion, the communicant bows his or her head before the Sacrament as a gesture of reverence and receives the Body of the Lord from the minister." See also RS, 90. The posture of standing to receive Holy Communion is very much in keeping with the way other liturgical processions take place, for example, there are entrance processions, processions with the gifts of bread and wine, Eucharistic processions, Palm Sunday processions, processions with the cross on Good Friday, and the procession with the Paschal candle at the Easter Vigil. Even the singing of the Communion antiphon, chant, or song is "to express the spiritual union of the communicants by means of the unity of their voices, to show gladness of heart, and to bring out more clearly the 'communitarian' character of the procession to receive the Eucharist'"(GIRM, 86).

17. See RS, 91.

18. See ibid., 92, 94.

19. See ibid., 92; Code of Canon Law, canon 1367.

20. NDRHC, 46.

21. See pages 37 and 52 for more information about low-gluten hosts.

22. "No other person, not even if he be a priest, may, on his own, add, remove, or change anything in the liturgy" (CSL, 22 § 3).

23. See NDRHC, 51–53; see also GIRM, 163, 182.

24. NDRHC, 52.

25. "As ordinary ministers of Holy Communion, the priest and the deacon purify the sacred vessels. The instituted acolyte, by reason of his office, 'helps the priest or deacon to purify and arrange the sacred vessels.' In the dioceses of the United States of America, the ministry of instituted acolyte, which is open only to men, is primarily made up of those preparing to receive Holy Orders. . . . An extraordinary minister of Holy Communion may not assist in the purification of sacred vessels" ("Seven Questions on the Distribution of Holy Communion Under Both Kinds," available from http://www.usccbpublishing.org/client/client_pdfs/SevenQuestions.pdf; accessed December 4, 2012).

26. BB, 1875.

27. LTP currently publishes a helpful annual resource specifically for extraordinary ministers who visit the sick and homebound. *The Catholic Handbook for Visiting the Sick and Homebound* includes these rites as well as the Gospel readings for Sundays and Holydays of Obligation. The pastoral introduction to this resource, written by S. Genevieve Glen, osb, is extremely helpful for preparing services with the sick and homebound.

28. *Pastoral Care of the Sick: Rites of Anointing and Viaticum* (PCS), 93.

29. See GIRM, 280.

30. See page 43.

31. See GIRM, 280.

32. Note that the sacred linens used to absorb the Precious Blood should be first washed by hand in water that is then poured down the sacrarium or suitably into the ground prior to a second washing in a regular way (see RS, 120).

33. The GIRM is very specific about these rubrics: "If Communion from the chalice is carried out by intinction, each communicant, holding a Communion plate under the mouth, approaches the Priest who holds a vessel with the sacred particles, with a minister standing at his side and holding the chalice. The Priest takes a host, intincts it partly in the chalice and, showing it, says *The Body and Blood of Christ.* The communicant replies, *Amen*, receives the Sacrament in the mouth from the Priest, and then withdraws" (GIRM, 287). Only a bishop or a priest may administer Holy Communion by intinction. It is not permitted for a deacon, a duly instituted acolyte, or an extraordinary minister to administer Holy Communion in this manner.

34. See http://www.vatican.va/holy_father/benedict_xvi/homilies/2005/documents/hf_ben-xvi_hom_20050529_bari_en.html.

Frequently Asked Questions

1. *Where did the title extraordinary minister of Holy Communion come from? Why aren't we called Eucharistic Ministers?*

Extraordinary minister of Holy Communion is the proper term for our ministry, because the term "eucharistic minister" can apply to the priest or deacon as well as to the lay ministers. The term "extraordinary minister of Holy Communion" makes clear that we are "extraordinary," that is, out of the ordinary, while the deacon, priest, and bishop are the "ordinary" ministers of Holy Communion. It is a reminder that we serve in this capacity only when there are insufficient clergy to distribute Holy Communion.[1]

2. *What is the role of the deacon at Mass?*

While the Mass can be celebrated by the priest alone, when a deacon is present he has certain special tasks. In particular, he proclaims the Gospel during the Liturgy of the Word, and is minister of the chalice during the Liturgy of the Eucharist. His presence impacts the extraordinary ministers in various ways, since he is involved in the distribution of Holy Communion, normally as the minister of the chalice, as well as in the handing of ciboria and chalices to the extraordinary ministers.

The deacon is the minister of the chalice during the Liturgy of the Eucharist.

    Unlike priests, deacons do not concelebrate—only two deacons may serve as deacons at any given Mass, except at the ordination of deacons. If other deacons are present, they may also be included in the procession on solemn occasions.[2]

3. What is the sacrarium?

The sacrarium is a special sink in the sacristy that does not drain to the sewer, but directly into the ground beneath the church building. It is used for the rinsing of sacred vessels following their purification by the priest, deacon, or instituted acolyte, for the rinsing of altar linens, and for the disposal of soiled hosts after they have been completely dissolved in water. Usually the sacristan is the person to handle the sacrarium, but it is good for all extraordinary ministers to know where the sacrarium is—and why it is there![3]

4. How many extraordinary ministers should there be for Mass?

The number of extraordinary ministers at Mass depends, firstly, on how many ordinary ministers are present—the priest, the deacon, and any concelebrating priests. It depends, secondly, on the number of people in attendance at Mass. There should be enough ministers to ensure that the Communion Rite is not unduly prolonged. Numbers of extraordinary ministers will also vary depending on the architecture of the church and the number of distinct seating sections.

5. What about people with celiac disease or gluten intolerance? How do they receive Holy Communion?

Just as some people are unable to receive the Precious Blood because of health reasons, some who have been diagnosed with celiac disease or gluten intolerance are unable to receive ordinary hosts. Communion is complete under either form, though its fullest expression comes in receiving under both kinds.[4] Therefore, those with celiac disease may receive from the chalice only and still receive the whole Christ. More and more communities, however, are also offering low-gluten hosts. Church law requires that the host be made from wheat and water, without any added ingredients, such as rice. In recent years, special hosts have been developed that have very low gluten content. These hosts have been deemed safe for most people with gluten intolerance or celiac disease. (Read more here: http://www.usccb.org/prayer-and-worship/the-mass/order-of-mass /liturgy-of-the-eucharist/celiac-sprue-disease.cfm.) However, only the person suffering from celiac disease or gluten intolerance, in consultation with their doctor, can determine whether these low-gluten hosts are safe for them. Every effort should be made to ensure that each and every member of the community has access to the Eucharist. That means that even if Holy Communion is given under one kind, whenever possible, the chalice should be made available to those who are unable to receive the host. Talk to your pastor and ministry coordinator if this situation arises in your parish.

If low-gluten hosts are used in your community, special arrangements will need to be made for where the hosts are distributed, since they cannot be mixed with the regular hosts. Usually, a particular station is designated as the "low-gluten" station.

If a supplier advertises "gluten-free" hosts, be cautious and do not assume that they are approved for use in the Catholic Church. You can always consult your diocesan worship office to find approved suppliers for low-gluten hosts.

Those who are unable to tolerate alcohol and cannot receive from the chalice may receive permission from the local Ordinary to receive Holy Communion under the form of mustum, a special grape juice.

6. *What about giving Holy Communion in flu season?*

Because extraordinary ministers of Holy Communion come in close contact with people, and handle the Body and Blood of Christ, we need to take special care to avoid the possibility of spreading germs.

- Never serve when you are sick or when you feel you're "coming down with something." Arrange for a substitute and remember that your own health and that of others needs to come first. Wait to serve until you are completely better, even if you feel you are no longer infectious. A coughing, sneezing minister will be a distraction and a cause of concern to those who come forward for Holy Communion.

- When you are sick, abstain from receiving from the chalice. (Keep in mind, though, that even if someone appears to be sick and infectious, if they present themselves before you to receive Holy Communion, you should give them the Precious Blood.

- Wash your hands carefully before Mass. Avoid touching your face or coughing into your hands during Mass. You can also use a hand sanitizer following the Sign of Peace and before taking your place to receive Communion.

• Always be careful to wipe the lip of the chalice, both inside and outside the rim, after each communicant approaches the chalice, and then turn the chalice slightly (about a quarter-turn) before presenting the chalice again to the next communicant. This is a required part of the way we serve the Precious Blood, and it is a matter both of reverence and hygiene. After each communicant, move to a new part of the purificator, turning it over when necessary.

• In extreme cases, the parish priest or the local bishop may decide to suspend Communion from the chalice until the danger of spreading disease has passed.

7. *Who can receive Holy Communion? What if someone comes forward who I think shouldn't be receiving Communion?*

Only Catholics in good standing—that is, who are not aware of grave sin and who have fasted for one hour—can receive Holy Communion. Generally, those who are not Catholic or Christian may not receive Communion. The United States Conference of Catholic Bishops has a short, pastoral explanation of this that is available at their website and that may be reprinted in parish bulletins or worship aids: http://www.usccb.org/prayer-and-worship/the-mass/order-of-mass/liturgy-of-the-eucharist/guidelines-for-the-reception-of-communion.cfm. Remember that as lay ministers, we give to each and every person who comes forward to receive Holy Communion, without exception, unless we are specifically instructed by the priest to do something different. It makes our task simple—we do not have to "screen" the people coming forward; all we have to do is give.

If you have a concern about someone who is coming forward, talk to the priest after Mass.

8. *What exactly is the Eucharistic fast? Does it apply to the sick and homebound?*

The Eucharistic fast requires all Catholics to abstain from any food or drink except water and necessary medicine for one hour before receiving Holy Communion.[5] (Notice that the fast is measured from the time of reception of Communion, not from the beginning of Mass.) Over the years, the length of the Eucharistic fast has been shortened to allow greater access to Holy Communion.

While our fasting in Lent applies only to those old enough to participate, no such age limits are applied to the Eucharistic fast—it applies to everyone, young and old, who receives Holy Communion. The only exceptions made are for the hospitalized, the homebound, and any who care for them—including family, caregivers, or hospital professionals. "The elderly, the infirm, and those who care for them can receive the Most Holy Eucharist even if they have eaten something within the previous hour."[6] Some dioceses recommend an abbreviated fast even for people in these situations—check with your diocesan chancery to find out if this is the case in your community.

9. How often can I receive Holy Communion?

A Catholic who is not aware of grave sin, and who has observed the necessary fast, may receive Holy Communion a second time during Mass (outside of the danger of death). For example, if you attend a weekday Mass, a wedding Mass, or a funeral Mass on a Saturday morning, you can still participate in the anticipated Sunday Mass that evening, and you can receive Holy Communion at both Masses. But if both Masses are the same—for example, a morning Mass and an evening Mass on a Sunday or a Holyday of Obligation—then you can receive Holy Communion a second time.[7] Therefore, someone who serves at cantor at the 9:00AM Mass and extraordinary minister at 11:00AM. However, you and your ministry coordinator should work to make these situations as rare as possible. (If you are serving at more than one Mass on a Sunday, it is a sign that your parish needs more volunteers!) Any Catholic may receive Holy Communion even as a third time in one day as Viaticum (that is, in danger of death).

10. I've noticed that readers and altar servers are blessed before they begin their ministry, extraordinary ministers of Holy Communion are deputed. Does that mean our ministry is the most important one?

While the *Book of Blessings* (BB) provides a simple blessing for sacristans, ushers, readers, cantors, and altar servers, it includes a more extensive "Order for the Commissioning of Extraordinary Ministers of Holy Communion" for the EMHCs.[8] It is not because we are more important, but because of the importance of the Eucharist that the rite for deputing extraordinary ministers is so extensive. The Church wants to ensure that the Blessed Sacrament is always handled "with the utmost care and reverence."[9] Thus the rite reminds us of the requirements for the ministry: we must be "examples of Christian living in faith and conduct." We must "strive to grow in holiness." We must be "especially observant of the Lord's command to love"[10] our neighbor. The two questions we are asked demand of us a firm commitment to serve our community and to handle the Blessed Sacrament with tremendous care.

Each minister is deputed for a specific community. Just because you are deputed in your home parish does not mean that you can give Holy Communion anywhere you may go. In addition, many parishes require extraordinary ministers be deputed anew every few years or even every year.

> **11. I was at Mass in another parish and the priest simply asked anyone who was able to come and help distribute Holy Communion. A few people came forward, he said a prayer over them from the Missal, and that was that. Why didn't they have to go through training and preparation?**

Most of the time, those serving as extraordinary ministers of Holy Communion go through an extensive process of learning and reflection before they are deputed through the special rite in the *Book of Blessings*. But *The Roman Missal* provides a special "Rite of Deputing a Minister to Distribute Holy Communion on a Single Occasion" for instances when there are simply not enough ministers to serve the entire assembly. He blesses these extraordinary ministers with a simple prayer: "May the Lord bless ✛ you, / so that at this Mass you may minister / the Body and Blood of Christ / to your brothers and sisters."[11] They are deputed for one Mass only to meet a specific need.

> **12. Where the Precious Blood is offered, what does the Church say about suitable numbers of ciboria and chalices?**

Because each gathered faith community is decidedly different (large urban and small rural parishes, military, school, and hospital chapels; wedding, funeral, and retreat Masses), there is no set number for the quantity of ciboria and chalices (if used) needed to communicate all the faithful in good standing. In the distribution of Holy Communion under both species, however, the Catholic Church in the United States teaches that "a suitable number of ministers of Holy Communion are [to be] provided at each Mass. For Communion from the chalice, it is desirable that there be generally two ministers of the Precious Blood for each minister of the Body of Christ . . . ."[12] In this way, the distribution of Holy Communion will not be "unduly prolonged."

13. *What are the diocesan requirements for serving as an extraordinary minister?*

Most dioceses have written guidelines for who may serve as an extraordinary minister of Holy Communion. You can often find these guidelines on your diocesan website, and the coordinator of your ministry should be able to help you access them. In most dioceses, the requirements are the same: the ministry is open to any confirmed Catholic man or woman in good standing with the Church, with a love for the Eucharist and a heart for service. There are generally additional requirements for ministry in hospitals or nursing homes and to the homebound. These ministers will generally need to undergo a background check and additional training to ensure a safe environment both for the minister and those he or she serves.

14. *What is an instituted acolyte?*

While the term "acolyte" is often used as a synonym for "altar server," it has a more precise meaning as well. Before the reforms following the Second Vatican Council, "acolyte" was one of the minor orders, steps on the way to Holy Orders. With the reforms, the minor orders were suppressed, and "acolyte" is now considered a lay ministry. It is, however, limited to men and is usually conferred on candidates preparing for the priesthood or the diaconate; however, a layman may also become an "instituted acolyte" by being formally installed in this ministry by the bishop. In his ministry, the "instituted acolyte" is permitted to assist with the purification of the sacred vessels after Holy Communion as well as function as an extraordinary ministry of Holy Communion and altar server.

15. What are the Church's laws regarding Holy Communion?

The faithful have the right to the celebration of Mass and reception of the sacred species as the Church has determined in her laws, rubrics, and norms in an integral manner faithful to Church doctrines and magisterial teachings, so that unity—not factions or divisions—results.[13]

There are certain rubrics (procedures) given by the Church that must be followed by everyone. Some of these are universal law; others are local, especially diocesan laws or guidelines. As an extraordinary minister, you are expected to know both. As an extraordinary minister you will need to learn the rules of your diocesan bishop from your bishop's staff and/or your pastor and his staff. For the worldwide Latin Catholic Church, the *General Instruction of the Roman Missal* (GIRM) dictates what one may or may not do. This has been clarified further by the instruction *Redemptionis sacramentum,* (RS).

Nationally, our United States Conference of Catholic Bishops (USCCB) provides further explanations and guidelines, within its competency, for how certain procedures will be carried out. There are national adaptations (with the approval of the Apostolic See) to the GIRM. *Norms for the Distribution and Reception of Holy Communion under Both Kinds in the Dioceses of the United States of America* (NDRHC) presents the particular law for the United States in applying number 283 of the GIRM.[14] Bishops, priests, and all the Christian faithful in the Latin rite of the United States are required to follow these norms.

Finally, in this context of legal teaching, in addition to the United States Conference of Catholic Bishops, the diocesan bishop, as moderator, promoter, and guardian of liturgical life in his territory, determines norms for the ministry of the extraordinary minister and for the distribution of Communion under both kinds within his diocese.[15] Where such norms have been promulgated by the diocesan bishop, they must be observed "in churches of religious and at celebrations with small groups."[16] It is very important to learn, know, and put into practice the teaching of the local bishop. Besides your pastor, the diocesan worship office and any personnel charged with training extraordinary ministers will be able to assist you. Legal teachings aid our identity by structuring what we do and what we do not do.

16. What are the norms for receiving Holy Communion under both species?

GIRM, 85 states:

"It is most desirable that the faithful, just as the Priest himself is bound to do, receive the Lord's Body from hosts consecrated at the same Mass and that, in the cases where this is foreseen, they partake of the chalice (cf. no. 283), so that even by means of the signs Communion may stand out more clearly as a participation in the sacrifice actually being celebrated."

These "cases" are further stipulated in GIRM, 283:

"In addition to those cases given in the ritual books, Communion under both kinds is permitted for:

a) Priests who are not able to celebrate or concelebrate Mass;

b) the Deacon and others who perform some duty at the Mass;

c) members of communities at the Conventual Mass or the "community" Mass, along with seminarians, and all those engaged in a retreat or taking part in a spiritual or pastoral gathering.

"The Diocesan Bishop may establish norms for Communion under both kinds for his own diocese" (GIRM, 85).

"The Diocesan Bishop may establish norms for Communion under both kinds for his own diocese, which are also to be observed in churches of religious and at celebrations with small groups. The Diocesan Bishop is also given the faculty to permit Communion under both kinds whenever it may seem appropriate to the Priest to whom a community has been entrusted as its own shepherd, provided that the faithful have been well instructed and that there is no danger of profanation of the Sacrament or of the rite's becoming difficult because of the large number of participants or for some other cause.

"In all that pertains to Communion under both kinds, the *Norms for the Distribution and Reception of Holy Communion under Both Kinds in the Dioceses of the United States of America* are to be followed (particularly nos. 27–54)."

17. If I am deputed to serve as an extraordinary minister of Holy Communion at my parish, does that mean I can serve in other places, too—at school Masses in my Catholic high school, or the parish I sometimes go for weekday Mass?

Extraordinary ministers are deputed to assist with the distribution of Holy Communion in one community. They are usually deputed for a specified length of time, or even for a single liturgy. Because you are deputed only for your own community, you would need to be deputed again before you could serve as an extraordinary minister in another diocese, or even another parish or faith community within your diocese.

On some occasions, the priest may simply ask for volunteers to assist him in the distribution of Holy Communion, especially when there are more people present than expected, or when there are insufficient ministers. In these cases, even if you are not in your home parish, you can certainly volunteer since your training and skill would allow you to be of service.

18. What are the requirements for serving as an extraordinary minister of Holy Communion? Do you have to be a certain age? Do you have to be confirmed?

In the document creating the special role of extraordinary ministers of Holy Communion, *Immensae caritatis* (1973), the Congregation for Divine Worship and the Discipline of the Sacraments did not provide a minimum age for candidates, nor does the document specifically refer to the Sacrament of Confirmation. Instead, it simply specifies that candidates be "fit persons, each chosen by name as a special minister, in a given instance or for a set period or even permanently" (I). These "fit persons" may be seminarians, religious, catechists, or "one of the faithful —a man or a woman" (IV). They "must be persons whose good qualities of Christian life, faith, and morals recommend them. Let them strive to be worthy of this great office, foster their own devotion to the eucharist, and show an example to the rest of the faithful by their own devotion and reverence toward the most august sacrament of the altar. No one is to be chosen whose appointment the faithful might find disquieting" (VI).

While no age is stipulated, the Church envisions that extraordinary ministers are mature Catholics in good standing.

While the document does not specify the age of candidates for the ministry, or include reception of the Sacrament of Confirmation as a requirement, it is clear that the rite envisions the ministry being given to mature Catholics in good standing with the Church. Each local bishop is free to develop additional requirements to ensure that this vision is carried out. In many places, that means that only those who have been confirmed are deputed as extraordinary ministers. Your ministry coordinator will direct you to the guidelines in your own diocese.

NOTES

1. 1983 *Code of Canon Law* in canon 910, §2, states that "the extraordinary minister of holy communion is an acolyte or another member of the Christian faithful designated according to the norm of canon 230, §3." Canon 230 says the laity can lawfully supply the duty of someone to distribute Holy Communion. See also RS, 88, 147, 151, 154-156; GIRM, 100, 162, 284a; NDRHC, 28.

2. See GIRM, 94, 182, 284a; NDRHC, 26.

3. See GIRM, 334; NDRHC, 55.

4. See GIRM, 282; NDRHC, 15.

5. See canon 919 §1.

6. See canon 919 §3.

7. Canon 917.

8. The *Book of Blessings* uses the term "commissioned," but throughout this resource, the word "deputed" is used because this is the word used in the NDRHC, 28: "When

the size of the congregation or the incapacity of the bishop, Priest, or Deacon requires it, the celebrant may be assisted by other bishops, Priests, or Deacons. If such ordinary ministers of Holy Communion are not present, 'the Priest may call upon extraordinary ministers to assist him, that is, duly instituted acolytes or even other faithful who have been duly deputed for this purpose. In case of necessity, the Priest may depute suitable faithful for this single occasion (cf. GIRM, no. 162).'" *The General Instruction of the Roman Missal* also uses the word "deputed" in 100: "In the absence of an instituted acolyte, there may be deputed lay ministers to serve at the altar and assist the Priest and the Deacon; these carry the cross, the candles, the thurible, the bread, the wine, and the water, or who are even deputed to distribute Holy Communion as extraordinary ministers." See also GIRM, 162: "In the distribution of Communion the Priest may be assisted by other Priests who happen to be present. If such Priests are not present and there is a truly large number of communicants, the Priest may call upon extraordinary ministers to assist him, that is, duly instituted acolytes or even other faithful who have been duly deputed for this purpose. In case of necessity, the Priest may depute suitable faithful for this single occasion."

9. BB, 1876.

10. BB, 1875.

11. Appendix III, *The Roman Missal.*

12. NDRHC, 30.

13. See RS, 12.

14. See GIRM, 22, 283; RS, 19, 101–102; canons 368, 375, 381, 392; NDRHC, 24.

15. See GIRM, 283; see also NDRHC, 24.

16. GIRM, 283.

Resources

Church Documents

Constitution on the Sacred Liturgy (CSL). This first of the four constitutions of the Second Vatican Council was promulgated on December 4, 1963. It laid the groundwork for the reform of the liturgy, and is still one of the most important Church documents on liturgy. This document is available in *The Liturgy Documents: Volumes I, II, and III* from Liturgy Training Publications.

The General Instruction of the Roman Missal (GIRM). This document is often published separately but really forms the introduction to *The Roman Missal*. It explains in detail how the Mass should be celebrated, and includes detailed rubrics about the Communion Rite. It is indispensable reading for priests, deacons, and masters of ceremonies. Other liturgical ministers, especially extraordinary ministers of Holy Communion, will benefit from familiarity with this important document. The text is found in the Missal and is also available from LTP, *The Liturgy Documents, Volume One: Fifth Edition.*

Norms for the Distribution and Reception of Holy Communion under Both Kinds in the Dioceses of the United States of America. This document, prepared by the United States Conference of Catholic Bishops in 2001, and approved by the Congregation for Divine Worship in 2002, is especially useful for extraordinary ministers of Holy Communion. It answers many basic questions about the do's and dont's of distributing Holy Communion. It also includes a strong theological background for the giving of Holy Communion under both kinds. The text is available in the Missal, online at http://old.usccb.org/liturgy/current/norms.shtml, and from LTP, *The Liturgy Documents, Volume One: Fifth Edition.*

Redemptionis sacramentum. This 2004 instruction from the Congregation for Divine Worship is a practical companion to *Ecclesia de Eucharistia,* the encyclical on the Eucharist by Blessed Pope John Paul II. It points to abuses around the celebration of the Eucharist. The document gives special attention to the various roles that may be filled by laypeople in the celebration of the Eucharist, and thus has some special relevance to extraordinary ministers. It is a helpful supplement to *The General Instruction of the Roman Missal.*

Ritual Texts

Pastoral Care of the Sick: Rites of Anointing and Viaticum. New York: Catholic Book Publishing Company, 1983. For any extraordinary minister working with the homebound, the hospitalized and those in care facilities, this book includes the rites to be followed in the distribution of Holy Communion, whether for a group or for an individual.

The Catholic Handbook for Visiting the Sick and Homebound. Chicago: Liturgy Training Publications, annual. This annual resource includes the official rites of the Church for the distribution of Holy Communion in Ordinary Circumstances as well as in a hospital or institutional setting. It includes the Sunday Gospel reading and the Gospel assigned to Holydays of Obligation for each liturgical year, allowing the extraordinary minister to bring the Word of God more fully to the people they serve.

A Ritual for Laypersons: Rites for Holy Communion and the Pastoral Care of the Sick and Dying. National Conference of Catholic Bishops. Committee on the Liturgy. Collegeville, Minnesota: The Liturgical Press, 1993. This small paperback is very useful for those who give Holy Communion outside of Mass, whether in the parish or in a hospital or nursing home. It also includes the pastoral care of the sick, and prayers for the dying and the dead.

Order for the Solemn Exposition of the Holy Eucharist. National Conference of Catholic Bishops. Bishops' Committee on the Liturgy. Collegeville, Minnesota: The Liturgical Press, 1993. At times, in the absence of a priest or deacon, the extraordinary minister of Holy Communion may be called on to preside at the exposition and/or reposition of the Blessed Sacrament, or at a Eucharistic service of Prayer and Praise during adoration of the Blessed Sacrament. This ritual book includes guidelines for laypeople presiding at such services.

Sunday Celebrations in the Absence of a Priest. United States Conference of Catholic Bishops. Committee on Divine Worship. Collegeville, Minnesota: The Liturgical Press, 1997; revised 2012. In the absence of a priest or deacon, an extraordinary minister of Holy Communion may be called on to preside at a liturgical service on a Sunday. This ritual text includes the complete prayers to be used for Morning or Evening Prayer with the distribution of Holy Communion and for the Celebration of the Liturgy of the Word with Holy Communion. It also includes helpful information for those called upon to lead or assist at such services. This resource, like all others, should always be used in conjunction with local diocesan guidelines.

Other References

Catechism of the Catholic Church. The *Catechism* is the indispensable resource on the teaching of the Church. It is structured as an exploration of three key texts: the Nicene Creed, the Ten Commandments, and the Lord's Prayer. The exhaustive index helps you to find quickly what the Church believes and teaches on an incredible range of topics. *The Compendium of the Catechism* is a synthesis of the *Catechism*, in question-and-answer format.

Huels, John M., JCD. *The Pastoral Companion: A Canon Law Handbook for Catholic Ministry, Fourth Edition.* Librairie Wilson & Lafleur Limitee, 2009. Intended especially for parish staff, this practical, hands-on book helps explain how Church law is lived out in day-to-day parish life.

The Mass and the Eucharist

Dies Domini: The Day of the Lord. May 31, 1998. This document (apostolic letter) of John Paul II focuses thematically on the primacy of the Resurrection of the Lord and how each Sunday is a weekly Easter; on

Sunday, the Lord's Day, as the day of Resurrection and victory; and on a richer appreciation of the Eucharistic assembly. Available from LTP in *The Liturgy Documents, Volume One: Fifth Edition.*

Driscoll, Jeremy, osb. *What Happens at Mass, Revised Edition.* Chicago, Illinois: Liturgy Training Publications, 2011. A profound reflection on what happens every time Mass is celebrated, exploring how God is acting through the liturgy, and how we are drawn into relationship with God and one another. The work examines the ritual words and actions in the Mass section by section.

Lukefahr, Oscar, cm. *We Worship: A Guide to the Catholic Mass.* Liguori, Missouri: Liguori, 2004. This book by a frequent parish mission director is intended to awaken us to the mystery of the Mass and to reignite "Eucharistic amazement" within us.

Nouwen, Henri J. M. *Can You Drink the Cup?* Notre Dame, Indiana: Ave Maria Press, 1996. This little book from a noted spiritual master takes Matthew 20:20–23 as a starting point for a meditation on the cup of salvation. The cup becomes the model for our Christian lives, for we are all called to hold the cup, lift the cup, and drink from the cup that is Christ.

Turner, Paul. *At the Supper of the Lamb: A Pastoral and Theological Commentary on the Mass.* Chicago, Illinois: Liturgy Training Publications, 2011. This book walks you through each part of the Mass. Its structure follows the Order of Mass as given in the third edition of *The Roman Missal.* This book is an invitation to worship, a call to new intention, and a deeper awareness of the privilege we share to be invited to the supper of the Lamb.

Turner, Paul. *A Guide to the General Instruction of the Roman Missal, Second Edition.* Chicago, Illinois: Liturgy Training Publications, 2011. A simple and concise aid to understanding *The General Instruction of the Roman Missal* and how it relates to the mystery of the Mass and Christ's sacrifice and the minister's participation.

Glossary

ALB: A long, white garment, worn by priests, deacons, and by lay ministers as well. It is a reminder of the white garment given in Baptism.

APOSTOLIC SEE: The Episcopal see of Rome. The pope as bishop of Rome has supreme authority over the regulation of the liturgy.

BENEDICTION: A blessing given by a priest with the Blessed Sacrament exposed in a monstrance.

BLESSED SACRAMENT: The name commonly used to refer to the Eucharistic elements of bread and wine after they have been consecrated and have become the Body and Blood of Christ. The term may also be used to refer to the consecrated bread alone.

CELIAC SPRUE DISEASE: Those affected by celiac sprue disease cannot ingest gluten from wheat without becoming ill.

CHALICE: The cup, usually with a stem, used to hold the wine to be consecrated at Mass. Sometimes also called a "communion cup."

CIBORIUM (PLURAL CIBORIA): The sacred vessel, usually with a cover, that holds the hosts for the distribution of Holy Communion and to store the consecrated hosts in the tabernacle. These vessels are usually either bowl or chalice-like in shape. They are usually made from metal and should be unbreakable.[1]

CINCTURE: A belt, usually white, which is sometimes worn with an alb.

COMMUNICANT: Any person who receives Holy Communion.

COMMUNION RITE: The Communion Rite is the last part of the Liturgy of the Eucharist. It begins with the Lord's Prayer, and includes the Sign of Peace, the Lamb of God, during which the fraction of the host takes place, and the distribution of Communion to the faithful. The Communion Rite ends with the Prayer after Communion.

CONSECRATED: Refers to the bread and wine that have become the Body and Blood of Christ during Mass. When the priest prays the words of Jesus in the consecration, the bread and wine cease to be bread and wine (although the appearance of bread and wine remain); they become and Body and Blood of Christ.

CONSECRATION: Refers to the narrative of the Institution of the Eucharist in the Eucharistic Prayer, where the priest pronounces the words of Christ at the Last Supper and the bread and wine are transformed into the Body and Blood of Christ.

CORPORAL: The square white, linen cloth placed on top of the altar cloth upon which any chalices and ciboria are placed during the celebration of Mass. Any vessels (chalice, ciborium, monstrance) holding the Blessed Sacrament are to be placed on a corporal.

CREDENCE TABLE: A table in the sanctuary on which the wine and water cruets, water basin/pitcher, and towel are placed for the celebration of Mass.

DEPUTED: This term refers to a public act of installing and blessing a member of the laity into a non-ordained ministry of service for either a single or multiple occasion(s). It is specifically used in reference to extraordinary ministers of Holy Communion.

EXPOSITION: A rite in which a consecrated host is "exposed," that is, displayed, for public veneration in a monstrance.

EUCHARISTIC SPECIES: The consecrated Body and Blood of Christ. Also called the sacred species.

EXTRAORDINARY MINISTER OF HOLY COMMUNION: A non-ordained person who is deputed to distribute the Body and Blood of Christ for either a single Mass or on multiple occasions.

INDULT: A concession or favor granted by the lawful superior (pope, Apostolic See, bishop) that allows the recipient to do something that the common law of the Church may not otherwise permit.

INSTITUTED ACOLYTE: A ministry of service to assist at the altar primarily by preparing the altar and sacred vessels for Mass. The acolyte may carry the cross in procession, present the book to and assist the priest or the deacon in the Preparation of the Altar and the Gifts and throughout the Mass as needed, serve as an extraordinary minister of Holy Communion if necessary, and assist with the purification of the sacred vessels.[2] Only men may be formally instituted acolytes. Although this ministry may exist on its own, most often it is a transitional ministry conferred on candidates for ordination as deacon or priest.

INTINCTION: A method of receiving Holy Communion in which the priest dips the consecrated host into the Precious Blood, says "The Body and Blood of Christ," and places it directly on the tongue of the communicant. Only a priest or a bishop may distribute Holy Communion in this manner.

LECTIONARY FOR MASS: The series of books that contain the readings used during Mass.

LITURGY: From the Greek *leitourgia*, originally meaning "a public act" (the "work of the people") performed for the good of the community. In the Roman Catholic Church, the word is used in reference to any of the official rites of the Church as found in the Roman ritual book. This would include, for example, Mass, the Liturgy of the Hours, Word services, and celebrations of the sacraments.

LITURGY OF THE EUCHARIST: Begins with the Preparation of the Altar and the Gifts following the Liturgy of the Word, and includes the Eucharistic Prayer, Communion Rite, and Prayer after Communion.

LITURGY OF THE HOURS: Called "the prayer of the Church with Christ and to Christ,"[3] the primary offices of the Liturgy of the Hours are Morning Prayer and Evening Prayer. It consists largely of the chanting or recitation of psalms. It is prayed daily by bishops, priests, religious, deacons, and many laypeople.

LITURGY OF THE WORD: The part of Mass from the First Reading through the Universal Prayer (Prayer of the Faithful) during which the action of Mass is focused on the ambo or pulpit.

MONSTRANCE: A sacred vessel that exposes a consecrated host to the faithful for adoration within church or during a procession, above all on the Solemnity of the Most Holy Body and Blood of Christ (Corpus Christi).

NAVE: The main body of a church, so called from its imagined resemblance to a ship.

ORDINARY MINISTER OF HOLY COMMUNION: Those who have received the Sacrament of Holy Orders (bishop, priests, and deacons).

PALL: A small, square, cloth-covered board, which may be used to cover the chalice to keep insects out. Its use is now optional. The term also refers to the white cloth used to cover the coffin of the deceased during the Funeral Liturgy. It is a reminder of the baptismal garment.

PATEN: The name for the plate used to hold the Eucharistic bread. Although the term is especially associated with the small plate used to hold the host for the priest, it can also be applied to a larger plate containing a sufficient number of hosts for the communion of the entire assembly. A ciborium, which is more like a cup or bowl in shape, can also be used to distribute hosts, and especially to store them in the tabernacle.

PURIFICATION: The pouring of water (or water and wine) into the sacred vessels to cleanse them of loose particles of the host and remove any remaining Precious Blood. After the liquid is consumed, a purificator is used to dry the sacred vessels. The purification of sacred vessels is limited to the ordained and to instituted acolytes.

PURIFICATOR: A small, absorbent, preferably white, easily laundered cloth used for cleaning the chalice(s) during Mass by wiping the lip of the chalice and, either after Holy Communion or after Mass, to dry all the sacred vessels during the purification process.

PYX: A small round vessel, often shaped like pocket watch, in which the consecrated host is carried to the sick, homebound, and dying.

ROMAN MISSAL: Formerly called *The Sacramentary*. The liturgical book that contains the rubrics and prayers for the celebration of the Mass according to the Roman Rite.

RUBRIC: The rules, guidelines and directions to be followed in the celebration of Mass and other liturgical rites. Because these instructions or guidelines are usually printed in red in the Missal, they came to be called "rubrics" from the Latin, *ruber*, meaning red.

SACRARIUM: A sink emptying directly into the ground, not the sewer, which is used for the rinsing of sacred vessels after their purification, for the first washings of corporals and purificators, or the water containing the completely dissolved consecrated hosts that cannot properly be consumed.

SACRED SPECIES: The consecrated Body and Blood of Christ. Same as Eucharistic species.

SACRED VESSEL: Refers to any receptacle used for holding the bread and wine to be consecrated at the Mass, and includes patens, chalices, and ciboria, usually made of gold or precious metal. In the United States vessels may be made from other solid, precious material that is suitable for sacred use and is not easily broken or found deteriorating.[4] These objects are blessed.

SANCTUARY: That area of the church building that contains the altar, ambo, and presidential chair.

TABERNACLE: An immovable, locked receptacle in which the Body of Christ is reserved in the church. A sanctuary lamp, whether of wax or oil, is placed nearby.[5]

THURIBLE: Also called a censer. A vessel for carrying incense in procession. It is usually made of metal and hangs from a chain.

TRANSEPTS: Side aisles in a cruciform-shaped church.

NOTES

1. See GIRM, 329.

2. See GIRM, 187-193.

3. *General Instruction of the Liturgy of the Hours* (GILOH), 2.

4. See GIRM, 329.

5. See GIRM, 314.

Acknowledgments

Prayer of Preparation

Bread of life, Jesus Christ,
you shed your blood to save us.
May your Spirit fill my heart
that I may love as you do love
all those I serve at Mass today.
Amen.